THE CHRISTIAN SCIENCE MYTH

By WALTER R. MARTIN
and NORMAN H. KLANN

With a great deal of research, the entire doctrine of Christian Science is thoroughly discussed and exposed in the pages of this book. A survey of the life of its founder, Mary Baker Eddy, and frequent quotations from her writings and those of other Christian Scientists are laid parallel to the life of Jesus Christ and the words of Holy Scripture. The growth of the Christian Science church as a powerful organization, as well as 'so-called' cures of its practitioners, among other events, are carefully chronicled. In light of the compiled information the whole cult and its doctrine are exploded as false.

The Wartburg Press says, "The authors take apart the myth of Mrs. Eddy, and show how Christian Science is deficient both in Christian faith and scientific basis. It sets up the theology of the Christian Scientists and offers refutation to it. It points out the power behind Christian Science censorship and analyzes the claimed cures of this cult. The work is thorough and should prove helpful to Christians everywhere."

The Christian Science Myth

by

WALTER R. MARTIN
AND
NORMAN H. KLANN

Published by
ZONDERVAN PUBLISHING HOUSE
Grand Rapids, Michigan

The Christian Science Myth

Copyright 1955
by Walter R. Martin
Paterson, New Jersey

Published by arrangement with
Biblical Truth Publishing Society, Inc.

First printing, April 1955
Second printing, September 1955
Third printing (Revised and Enlarged), December 1955

Printed in the United States of America

16622

FOREWORD

Why should a book like this be written? There are some people who object to anything that is a criticism of another person's religion. They have various forms of criticism: "Aren't all religions good?" "Don't you believe in freedom of religion?" "Why don't you just preach positively and let the truth take care of itself?" "Should you say anything that might hurt someone's feelings?"

The follower of the Lord Jesus Christ can have but one answer to these questions. We are not free to choose our message nor are we free to choose our methods. We must obey the Word of God and follow Christ in His example.

Jesus Christ was the most tolerant Man who ever lived on this earth, but He was also the most intransigent. He showed that each man could do as he pleased but He taught that anyone who did not do what He said would be sent to Hell for it. Those words may seem blunt but even a cursory reading of the four gospels will show that they are true.

The woman at the well had her sin revealed to her and tried to change the subject by leading Christ into a religious argument. Religion has often been a fox-hole into which the aroused soul plunges in order to protect itself from the terrible conviction which the Holy Spirit brings to the guilty one. She reminded Christ that the Samaritans sacrificed to their god on Mount Gerazim while the Jews offered their sacrifices to Jehovah in Jerusalem. Who was right? Emily Post and Mrs. Mary Baker Eddy would probably agree that the proper answer should be a broad, smooth compromise that would leave each person free to decide for himself or herself. Christ was not bound by etiquette. His answer was devastating and serves as a model for all who would follow Him. "Woman," he told her, "you worship you know not what;

we know what we worship; for salvation is of the Jews" (John 4:22). This was an appeal, of course, to the seventeenth chapter of Leviticus where God had plainly said that there should be no sacrifice except at the door of the tabernacle of the congregation. Here is the establishment of the divine rule for religious freedom: Every man has a right to go to Hell in his own way or to go to Heaven in God's way.

In *Science and Health,* the key that locks the Scriptures so that they can be twisted to Satan's ends, Mrs. Eddy makes many mis-quotations and mis-applications. She calls Christ, for example, "the Way-shower." If you go outside of your city and see a way-shower which reads "Fifty miles to Next-town," you don't climb up the sign, you follow the road. Christ was not the way-shower; He was and is the Way.

In another place Mrs. Eddy says that Satan is a lie, and that a lie is unreality, and that therefore Satan is unreality, and therefore he does not exist. But Christ did not say that Satan was a lie, but rather that he is a liar. There is a vast difference between a lie and a liar. "You are of your father the Devil," Jesus said to those who had made themselves His enemies. "The lusts of your father you will do. He was a murderer from the beginning, and abode not in the truth, because there is no truth in him. When he speaks a lie, he is using something that is particularly his own; for he is a liar and the father of it" (John 8:44).

That this system has no science in it is evident from its attitude toward disease. It attempts to say that sickness, suffering, and death are unreality. Its famed newspaper, the *Christian Science Monitor,* seldom uses the word death in its stories. When every other newspaper in the world reported the death of Franklin D. Roosevelt, the *Monitor* headlined, "Truman Succeeds to the Presidency." Not until ten inches down the column was there a reference to Roosevelt. Then the article got near to the truth by beginning a paragraph, "With the passing of the late President . . ."

4

In a conversation with a total stranger, I identified her after a few sentences as a member of the Christian Science group. She was astounded, and wanted to know how I knew. I replied, "You said that your husband 'passed on.' In fact what happened was that he died." It was the entering wedge for me to give the testimony of life in Christ.

There are many instances on record of heartless cruelty to children by the members of this sect. Stupified with their unscientific belief about sickness they have failed to call physicians in times of emergency and have allowed innocent people to suffer horribly while they attempted to "demonstrate science" by giving the sick one "absent treatment."

In the state of Georgia a few years ago a law was introduced requiring all applicants for marriage licenses to obtain certificates showing their freedom from venereal disease. A Christian Scientist introduced an amendment that would have freed members of the Christian Science churches from this requirement. Needless to say the amendment was defeated. One of the legislators remarked that a spirochete had no religion.

Finally, it should be realized that this book will be received with hatred, denials and illegality by the followers of this false prophetess. At a convention of the American Library Association recently it was reported by librarians that books criticizing Christian Science were constantly stolen from the shelves of public libraries in the United States. This system, like many other false religions, is a glowworm which has need of the darkness in order to shine.

If there is any reader who has been enmeshed in *Science and Health* who wishes to put it to a real test, let him be willing to put the book aside and not touch it for six months. Let him take up the Bible and read nothing but the Word of God for half a year and surrender himself to the reading from moment to moment. One who is willing to do this will find that "the entrance of thy words giveth light" (Ps. 119:130).

If any true Christian has anything to do with a follower of Mrs. Eddy, do not fail to deal with such with a great manifestation of the love of Jesus Christ for these who are carried captive by Satan at his will. Poor souls, poor *blind* souls—see if you can't show them the true love of Christ flowing through you. Thus with the light of the Word and the love of the believer, they may be brought to the true Lord Jesus Christ, the eternal second person of the Godhead, the Saviour who gave Himself a ransom for all.

The late Bishop J. Taylor Smith, of the Church of England, visited America a few years before his death and upon his return to England he was asked what he thought of America. He answered, "Very wonderful and very curious." Someone wanted him to illustrate his reply and he answered, "Wonderful? Niagara Falls, the Grand Canyon, and the whole people. Curious? Grape-nuts and Christian Science. They have a breakfast food which they call grape-nuts and it has in it neither grapes nor nuts. They have a religion which they call Christian Science and it has in it neither Christianity nor science."

DONALD GREY BARNHOUSE

PREFACE

Unlike other non-Christian religions and cults, Christian Science is unique, in that it demands of its adherents that they be unswervingly loyal to their founder and "Leader," Mary Baker Eddy. The story of this unusual and mysterious woman will unfold before the reader as he further peruses this book, but a few introductory comments are, we believe, in order.

One cannot open any textbook on or about Christian Science without encountering the writings, sayings or influence of Mrs. Eddy. She stands paramount above every detail that Christian Science portrays; indeed Christian Science is, in a word, Mary Baker Eddy. Beyond a doubt Mormonism had its prophet, Joseph Smith, and his disciple, Brigham Young; Theosophy had Madam Blavatsky; Unity was represented by the Fillmores; while Seventh-Day Adventism gave to the world Ellen G. White, but while the dominating influence of their writings has for the most part faded into the shadows of time, Mrs. Eddy continues to reign supreme and unrivaled, a hollow queen from beyond the grave.

Most cult members become intensely disturbed when the various founders of their systems are condemned and their teachings refuted. Christian Scientists therefore protest strongly the truth about Mrs. Eddy and *her* religion. They loudly insist that she has been the victim of malicious slander on the part of her jealous enemies, and do not hesitate to picture her as the greatest religious personality on the horizon of history since the advent of the Son of God. Mrs. Eddy, or "Our Beloved Leader," as the faithful Scientists refer to her, never blushed at such tributes, modesty never having been one of her strong virtues. Quite to the contrary, "Mother Eddy" claimed not only that she was inspired by God but that *He,*

7

not she, was responsible for her book, *Science and Health, With Key to the Scriptures,* one of the most controversial books of the last century.

The authors of this book, as the bibliography will reveal, have left nothing to chance in their investigation of either Mrs. Eddy or her religion and have considered all available sources, both for and against, in this endeavor. It is not our desire to attack any Christian Scientist personally or to distort the truth of history in this survey. We only desire to analyze as objectively as possible the evidence as it presents itself from all reliable channels. Hence facts and only facts are the subject of this study.[1] It is then in the interests of the *whole* truth that this work is presented that all may clearly see the true and unvarnished character of Mary Baker Eddy and the Christian Science religion.

The authors realize full well that much adverse criticism will come from Christian Scientists who violently challenge any attempts to honestly present the saga of Mrs. Eddy, and also from those who will seek to compare this effort with far more extensive biographical material already in print. To offset these two major points of expected comment we should therefore like to make plain our intentions. This book is not intended to be a competitive effort where biography is concerned, or for that matter is it represented as a substitute for such superb works now in existence. Rather, this work is designed as a survey of the Christian Science founder and her religion, embodying what the authors consider the historical, philosophical and theological propositions which best portray the evolution of the Eddy philosophy.

The authors wish to acknowledge their sincere debt of gratitude to Edwin Franden Dakin, Georgine Milmine, Sibyl

---

[1]However, in all fairness the authors must admit that where Mrs. Eddy and Christian Science are concerned theological objectivity is virtually impossible since the perversions of the system are in no sense capable of being evaluated from a Christian standpoint *except* critically.

CHAPTER I

THE ORIGIN AND HISTORY OF CHRISTIAN SCIENCE

Throughout the length and breadth of America and count-less other nations today, the Churches of Christ Scientist are to be seen in ever-increasing numbers. The wealth and prestige shared by Christian Scientists is difficult to evaluate, especially their propaganda machinery amply supplemented by the *Christian Science Monitor* of Boston.

Generally speaking, the adherents of Christian Science are well-dressed, clean-cut, and to all appearances intelligent persons with incomes above the average level. Their churches are well-kept and expensively furnished and many of them, if not all, are equipped with reading rooms where Mrs. Eddy's literature is conspicuously in evidence. The majority of Christian Scientists are apparently happy in their religion (*Science*). About this there can be little doubt. And they vigorously defend it and Mrs. Eddy whenever it is deemed advantageous to do so. The evolution of Christian Science has therefore brought it what Mrs. Eddy could never endow it with—namely, its acceptance by many as a nominally Christian sect. This, then, is the over-all portrait of Christian Science activity to the indifferent minds of so many Christians—but a far different picture awaits us as we turn back the hands of time to its origin and development from the pens of Phineas Parkhurst Quimby and Mary Baker Eddy.

Like the sword of Damocles, the name "Quimby" has hung over the history of Christian Science since Mrs. Eddy first claimed she authored the system and originated the principles upon which it stands. "Dr." Quimby* has been alternately

---

*Phineas P. Quimby was an ardent admirer of Franz Anton Mesmer and, though poorly educated, absorbed many of Mesmer's ideas relative to "suggestion" and hypnotism.

praised and damned over a period of seventy-five years by
most Christian Scientists who bother to investigate the claims
of Mrs. Eddy. But who is this man of mystery that Christian
Scientists would like to bury under an avalanche of subtle
propaganda? What part does he play in the Christian Science
melodrama? Why is he important enough to be feared? These
questions can now be candidly answered in their entirety and
they cannot any longer be concealed or ignored.

Phineas Parkhurst Quimby,[1] the father of Christian
Science, was born in Lebanon, New Hampshire, February 16,
1802, and moved to Belfast, Maine, in 1804. He spent all of
his life in that community up until 1859 when his "practice"
compelled him to expand to Portland, Maine. "Dr." Quimby,
as he was known, became embroiled in mesmerism early in
his life and after connecting this phase of activity with an
assortment of religious terms and adding a dash of psychology
graduated into a full-fledged "mental healer." Denying the
principle that matter has reality, Quimby built up a considerable following, having authored numerous articles and manuscripts dealing with his theories.

"Dr." Quimby in the late 1850's had already discovered
his "Science of Man,"[2] (see Chapter IX), which manuscript
was used by Mrs. Eddy and sections of which she reworded
and incorporated into "her" textbook, *Science and Health,
With Key to the Scriptures.* Quimby spoke of his system as "The
Science of The Christ." Mrs. Eddy went him one better and
made it *Christian Science,* considerably after his demise, however, thereby eliminating any possibility of Quimby exposing
her.[3] It is therefore easily shown that Quimby used the name
"Christian Science" before Mrs. Eddy "discovered" it. Mrs.
Eddy's many followers, of course, vehemently deny these facts,

[1] *The Quimby Manuscripts,* Horatio Dresser, p. 2.
[2] *The Religio-Medical Masquerade,* F. W. Peabody, pp. 91, 92.
[3] Quimby in 1863 called it "Christian Science," three to six years prior to Mrs.
Eddy's claim. Compare *Quimby Manuscripts,* p. 388.

but the weight of evidence is far too great to be so easily brushed aside. Let it not be assumed by anyone reading this that *Science and Health** is Quimby's book—far from it, but it is demonstrably true that Mrs. Eddy based her system upon his, plagiarized excerpts from his manuscripts and switched his terminology about to make up a major portion of her first literary effort. Mrs. Eddy herself repeatedly contradicts her own testimony as to how she "discovered" Christian Science, so let us consider her contradictions and then the verifiable facts, repugnant though they may be to ardent Scientists. In October, 1862 (four years before Quimby's death), Mary Baker Eddy (then Mary M. Patterson) committed herself to the care of P. P. Quimby in Portland, Maine, for treatment of "spinal inflammation." On November 7, 1862, she alleged that Quimby healed her of the infirmity. Mrs. Patterson said,

> I visited P. P. Quimby and in less than one week from that time I ascended by a stairway of 182 steps to the dome of the City Hall and am improving, ad infinitum.[4]

Following this acclaim for Quimby and his powers, Mrs. Patterson studied his manuscripts thoroughly and copied them extensively[5] over a three-week period which, via correspondence, stretched out to almost three years in the final analysis. Not only is this a matter of record, but from the years 1867 to 1870, *after* the death of Quimby, she edited, copied and taught *his* theories allowing that they were *his*, not hers! These same theories she published in 1875 thinly masked in remarkably similar language and titled *Science and Health, With Key to the Scriptures.*[6] Sworn statements of the persons with whom she boarded at this time are available to substantiate this. But

---

*Even this title Mrs. Eddy appropriated from Quimby with but the change of one word. Quimby called his ideas "Science of Health"—she entitled her book *Science and Health.* See—*The Quimby Manuscripts*, p. 389, edition 1921.

[4]*Portland Evening Courier.*

[5]*Quimby Manuscripts*, pp. 436-438.

[6]*Religio-Medical Masquerade*, pp. 82-83.

let us return to Mrs. Eddy's explanation of how she "discovered" Christian Science.

According to an authorized statement published by the Christian Science Publishing Society of Boston, Mrs. Eddy after a fall on a slippery sidewalk February 1, 1866, was pronounced "incurable" and given three days to live by the attending physician (Dr. Alvin M. Cushing). The third day, allegedly her last on earth, Mrs. Eddy (the statement makes out) cried for a Bible, read Matthew 9:2 and rose completely healed. Thus the statement claims "she discovered" Christian Science.

Corroborating this new story, Mrs. Eddy in her book, *Retrospection and Introspection,* declares that in February of 1866 (one month after Quimby's death), she was mortally injured in a sidewalk fall and was not expected to live. She, however, vanquished the angel of death in this skirmish, and on the third day emerged triumphant over her bodily infirmity. These two statements, the interested reader will note, substantiate each other in every detail; it is therefore most unfortunate that they should both be deliberate falsehoods. Mrs. Eddy never discovered Christian Science in the manner claimed, never was in danger of losing her life in the manner described, and never "rose the third day healed and free" as she maintained. Two incontrovertible facts establish these truths beyond doubt. They are as follows: (1) Dr. Alvin M. Cushing, the attending physician at this "illness" of Mrs. Eddy, denied under oath in a 1,000-word statement that he ever believed or said that she was in a precarious physical condition.* Moreover Dr. Cushing stated (contrary to the claims of Christian Scientists that Mrs. Eddy always enjoyed robust health) that he further attended her in August of the same year four separate times and administered medicine to her for bodily ailments. (2) Mr. Julius Dresser (pupil of the late "Dr."

---

*The authors have this statement in its entirety, should it ever be necessary to substantiate this fact further.

Quimby) received a letter from Mrs. Eddy dated February 15, 1866, two weeks *after* her alleged "recovery" from the fall on an icy sidewalk. In this letter Mrs. Eddy alludes to the fall and claims Dr. Cushing resigned her to the life of a cripple. Mrs. Eddy wrote:

> Two weeks ago I fell on the sidewalk and struck my back on the ice and was taken for dead, came to consciousness, admitted a storm of vapors from cologne, chloroform, ether, camphor, etc., but to find myself the helpless cripple I was before I saw Dr. Quimby. The physician attending said I had taken the last step I ever should but in two days I got out of my bed alone and will walk, but yet I confess I am frightened . . . now can't *you* help me? I think I could help another in my position . . . yet I am slowly failing. . . .°

Barring the obvious medical error of a doctor administering chloroform and ether to an unconscious person, Mrs. Eddy's account once again demonstrates her ability to think in paradoxes and contradict all reason and logical expression. The accounts are therefore spurious and complete fabrications.

Mr. Horace T. Wentworth, whose mother Mrs. Eddy lived with in Stoughton while she was teaching from the *Quimby Manuscripts* (1867-1870), has made the following statement, and no Christian Scientist has ever refuted it:

> As I have seen the amazing spread of this delusion and the way in which men and women are offering up money and the lives of their children to it, I have felt that it is a duty I owe to the public to make it known.
>
> I have no hard feelings against Mrs. Eddy, no axe to grind, no interest to serve; I simply feel that it is due the thousands of good people who have made Christian Science the anchorage of their souls and its founder the infallible guide of their daily life, to keep this no longer to myself. I desire only that people who take themselves and their helpless children into Christian Science shall do so with the full knowledge that this is not divine revelation but simply the idea of an old-time Maine healer.

Further than this statement Mr. Wentworth has also recorded as incontestable evidence the *very* copy of P. P. Quimby's *Manuscripts* from which Mrs. Eddy taught during the years 1867-1870, which copy also contains corrections in

°F. W. Peabody, *The Religio Medical Masquerade*, pp. 80-81.

Mrs. Eddy's *own* handwriting.* Note, please, all this is undeniable fact—yet Mrs. Eddy maintains that she *alone* "discovered and founded" the Christian Science religion. What an
historical perversion the prophetess of Christian Science has
attempted to perpetrate. Let it also be remembered that Mrs.
Eddy claimed for Quimby's theories, which she expanded,
Divine import, owning that she only copied what God Almighty spoke.[7] This subject will be further reviewed in Chapter IV, "The Christian Science Bible," so for the present in
this respect we shall allow Mrs. Eddy a brief respite from the
blinding searchlight of truth.

Let us return then to the personal history of the central
figure of this analysis, Mary Baker Eddy—the still reigning
Sovereign of Christian Science.

Mrs. Eddy first saw the light of day in Bow, New Hampshire, in the year 1821 as Mary Ann Morse Baker, youngest
daughter of Abigail** and Mark Baker, a "hard rock" New
Hampshire farmer. Mary Baker had three brothers and two
sisters, all of whom she survived by many years. In 1836
the Bakers moved to Tilton, New Hampshire, where the young
Mary was to grow up. The childhood of the future Mrs.
Eddy was anything but a pleasant one, marked continually
by a strange illness which seemed to grow in severity with
Mary's increasing years.[8] Young Mary, history tells us, was
quieted during these fits by rocking in a specially built cradle
made of an old sofa where she remained until she fell asleep.
As a small child she had often been subject to frequent fits
evidenced by a peculiar physical lethargy erupting into violent spasms of pronounced hysteria and ending eventually in
unconsciousness. Mary Baker was also plagued with a neurotic temper which exhibited itself whenever her wishes were

---

*Photostatic copies of this manuscript are also in the possession of the authors if
verification is desired.
[7]*Christian Science Journal*, January, 1901.
**Mrs. Baker died in 1849 and Mark Baker remarried shortly thereafter.
[8]E. F. Dakin, *Mrs. Eddy*, p. 19.

denied and her anger aroused.[9] Often the young girl would
roll upon the floor, scream, pound her feet, and usually termi-
nate the outburst by lapsing into unconsciousness. Couple, if
you will, this unfortunate psychological situation of chronic
hysteria with a strong New England religious background and
the emotional roots of the Christian Science religion begin to
take shape. Here was a young girl destined to suffer all her
life with such spasms[10] in varying intensities, and who neared
the end of her life with a legal test of her mental capacities
brought by her own sons, George W. Glover and Dr. Foster
Eddy. In fairness to Mrs. Eddy it must be noted that the
action was dropped and a large cash agreement ($300,000)
was made with her sons in 1909[*] to discourage further action.
Mrs. Eddy's clever advisers dared not allow her to attract
any more publicity than she already had, for unpleasant
publicity had already abounded beyond their wishes and to
the detriment of their church. Let us, however, continue our
study of Mrs. Eddy's personal background.

On December 11, 1843, at the age of 22, Mary Baker
married George W. Glover, the first of her three husbands and
her greatest love. Mary Glover's happiness, however, was
short-lived and her life marred not long after this union by
George Glover's untimely death of yellow fever in Wilming-
ton, S. C. She returned to New Hampshire a broken and
sickly woman about to bear her deceased husband's child.
It was after George W. Glover Junior's birth that Mrs. Eddy,
torn by bitter feelings and suffering from acute hysteria,
began her long association with the drug morphine.[11] Proof
that dependence upon morphine for treatment of her hysterical
spasms spanned her life, especially in the 1870's, is amply

---

[9]*Ibid*, pp. 6, 7.
[10]Georgine Milmine, *Life of Mary Baker Eddy*, pp. 21-35;
     E. F. Dakin, *Mrs. Eddy*, p. 10.
[*]Another suit was contemplated and although the "Next Friends" withdrew their
   case, this new action was planned and resulted in the settlement (see Dakin, *op. cit.*,
   pp. 455-460).
[11]*New York World*, October 30, 1906.

in evidence from incontrovertible sources[12] which are too lengthy to quote here, but it is a fact challenged by none but uninformed Christian Scientists. The authors are well prepared to prove this fact and have much evidence available, especially from the diary of Calvin Frye, who was for 25 years Mrs. Eddy's constant companion.

Mrs. Eddy's second marriage to Daniel M. Patterson, an amorous dentist (June 21, 1853), ended in divorce, Mrs. Eddy (then Mrs. Patterson) affirming that he was guilty of adultery though such a charge was never proved. Daniel Patterson was warned before his marriage to Mrs. Eddy (then Mrs. Glover) by no less an authority than her own father, Mark Baker, to the effect that his daughter Mary was a risky marital venture due to her "spells" of hysteria, and frequent temper. Nevertheless, Patterson went through with the marriage disregarding the sage advice of one who knew what the outcome would be, and dutifully carried his fiancée both up and down stairs, to and from the ceremony, for even at the beginning of their marriage Mary was recovering from one of her hysterical attacks.[13] To do justice to Mrs. Eddy in the matter of her divorce, let it be clearly understood that she was the innocent party in the Patterson case and therefore her morals and social actions can never be fairly challenged nor have they ever been impugned. She always enjoyed the reputation of puritanical morality and such derogatory allusions therefore by misinformed critics of Christian Science and Mrs. Eddy as to her marital life or status are for the most part grossly unfair and biased. She stands vindicated by all historical sources, at least where this matter is concerned.

The third and last marriage of Mary Baker Glover Patterson was vastly different from the first two and fortunately happier. In George Glover Mary Baker had found

---

[12]E. F. Dakin, *Mrs. Eddy*, pp. 19 and 149, and especially pp. 513 and 514; also *New York World*, May 8, 1907.

[13]E. F. Dakin, *Mrs. Eddy*, p. 29.

true romance and love, in Daniel Patterson, exciting masculinity, but in Asa Gilbert Eddy, whom she married in the autumn of her life, Mrs. Eddy found devotion and absolute resignation to her every wish. At last she had found a man meek enough to assuage her anger, tolerant enough to stomach her theology, and sick enough not to care what happened to Mrs. Eddy's metaphysical crusades. Asa Eddy suffered from a chronic heart condition which eventually killed him (June 30, 1882), although at his death Mrs. Eddy claimed he did not die of heart attack at all, but of "Malicious Mesmerism . . . I know it was poison that killed him, not material poison, but mesmeric poison."[14]

In a letter written to the *Boston Post* Mrs. Eddy made a desperate attempt to explain away her husband's death on the basis of mesmeric poison which she believed one of her ex-pupils directed against herself and Mr. Eddy. Indeed "Mental Malpractice" or "Malicious Animal Magnetism" (M. A. M. for short) dominated Mrs. Eddy as an unbridled obsession most of her life and was conveniently blamed for her own death by the Scientists of the day.

For the sake of clarity we have reproduced below excerpts from that letter which we believe will show clearly Mrs. Eddy's mental condition at its pitiful worst:

My husband's death was caused by Malicious Mesmerism. Dr. C. J. Eastman, who attended the case after it had taken an alarming turn, declares the symptoms to be the same as those of arsenic poisoning. On the other hand, Dr. Rufus K. Noyes, late of the City Hospital, who held an autopsy over the body today, affirms that the corpse is free from all material poison, although Dr. Eastman still holds to his original belief. I know it was poison that killed him, not material poison, but Mesmeric Poison. My husband was in uniform health—but seldom complained of any kind of ailment. During his brief illness, just preceding his death, his continual cry was, 'Only relieve me of this continual suggestion, through the mind, of poison, and I will recover . . .'

There was such a case in New York. Everyone at first declared poison to have been the cause of death, as the symptoms were all there;

but an autopsy contradicted the belief, and it was shown that the victim had had no opportunity for procuring poison. I afterwards learned that she had been very active in advocating the merits of our college. Oh, isn't it terrible, that this fiend of malpractice is in the land! . . . Circumstances barred me taking hold of my husband's case. He declared himself perfectly capable of carrying himself through, and I was so entirely absorbed in business that I permitted him to try, and when I awakened to the danger it was too late. . . . Today I sent for one of the students whom my husband had helped liberally, and given some money, not knowing how unworthy he was. I wished him to come, that I might prove to him how, by metaphysics, I could show the cause of my husband's death. He was as pale as a ghost when he came to the door, and refused to enter, or to believe that I knew what caused his death. Within half an hour after he left I felt the same attack that my husband felt—the same that caused his death. I instantly gave myself the same treatment that I had used in a case of arsenic poison, and so I recovered, just the same as I could have caused my husband to recover had I taken the case in time. After a certain amount of mesmeric poison has been administered it cannot be averted. No power of mind can resist it. . . . One of my students, a malpractitioner, has been heard to say that he would follow us to the grave. . . .

Here is the picture of an emotionally confused and frus-a woman who brazenly represented herself and her religion trated woman who frantically attempts to establish what is a medical absurdity, namely that Asa Eddy's heart was destroyed by "Mesmeric poison" directed at him by a metaphysical enemy (E. J. Arens by name). Three interesting facts can be gleaned from this letter which show how desperate Mrs. Eddy was over Asa's physical disproval of her theological claims. She who claimed to heal all manner of diseases could not heal her beloved husband, but merely whimpered at his bedside, "Gilbert, Gilbert, do not suffer so."[15] These words from as the successors to Jesus Christ in the field of healing, and who after witnessing and recognizing the suffering of her own husband, dared to write and teach that "there is no life, truth, intelligence or substance in matter, All is infinite Mind and its infinite manifestation, For God is All in all."[16] Mrs.

---

[15]Sibyl Wilbur, *Life of Mary Baker Eddy*, p. 279.
[16]Mary Baker Eddy, *Science and Health, With Key to the Scriptures*, 1914 edition, p. 468.

Eddy boldly taught that there is no sin, sickness or death and dogmatically affirmed the unreality of diseases and physical pain. Yet even after the autopsy when she beheld Asa's diseased heart, she dared to claim the cause of his death as a case of "mesmeric (mental) poison." The icy form of Asa G. Eddy should have silenced forever her illogical and unscientific philosophy of religion, and driven her to repentance toward God and faith in the real Saviour of mankind—not Christian Science, but the Son of God.

Secondly, Mrs. Eddy by demanding a post-mortem examination of Asa contradicted her own writings where she plainly states "a metaphysician never gives medicine, recommends or trusts in hygiene, or *believes in the ocular or post-mortem examination of patients.*"[17] Now if Mrs. Eddy practiced what she preached she should have abandoned Asa's remains to the scrap heap of mental malpractice and never investigated his demise, but the error was unavoidable since Mrs. Eddy was not to be outdone by any medical doctor. She was an expert healer by her own admission; the autopsy was therefore inevitable.

Thirdly, the name of "Dr." C. J. Eastman (Dean of the Bellevue Medical College) is conspicuous in the opening of her letter to the *Post*. This fact has interesting ramifications for a number of very sound reasons: (1) "Dr." Eastman held no medical degree or standing, and therefore his diagnostic opinions were worthless. (2) The college of which he was "Dean" was later proved to be a gigantic fraud and was closed as a false representative of the medical profession. (3) "Dr." Eastman, it was shown later, was illegally engaged in a virtual abortion mill for which offence he was subsequently sentenced to a five-year prison term. This was Mrs. Eddy's chief witness to her claim that Asa died of "metaphysical arsenic" (i.e., mesmeric poison). As a matter of

---

[17]*Science and Health*, edition 1881, p. 261.

easy cross reference, the interested reader will find that Sibyl
Wilbur's biography of Mrs. Eddy (the officially approved
work of the Christian Science Church) on page 270 attempts
to justify this unheard-of diagnosis. Wrote Miss Wilbur,

> Who can with authority deny Mrs. Eddy's statement that poison
> mentally administered killed her husband? "Not material poison," she
> declared, but "mesmeric poison."

Medical science, in answer to Miss Wilbur, speaks most
authoritatively and declares that such a psychological proposition carried to its logical conclusion borders on acute paranoia
and is a physical impossibility. However, it is a good barom-
eter as to how Christian Scientists think where Mrs. Eddy
is concerned. As an aside, it might also be noted that Mrs.
Eddy herself has been diagnosed by experts of the medical
profession as a pronounced paranoiac, seemingly incapable
of sound reasoning in many phases of mental operation.

Why Mrs. Eddy, displeased as she was, did not remain
silent when the weight of evidence against her was so over-
powering, no one will ever know, but a clue to her psychology,
and hence the probable reason, is to be found in a statement
the late Mr. Eddy made some years before his death. Quoth
the timorous Asa in a moment of reckless courage, "Mrs. Eddy
could not be pleased by God Almighty Himself." From such
an intimate authority, the authors can do little more than
defer in mute agreement. But let us further consider the
historical background of the Christian Science movement.

From the home of the Wentworths in Stoughton, Massachusetts, where she taught from the Quimby manuscripts Mrs.
Eddy went on to Lynn, Massachusetts, where she completed
her "writing" of *Science and Health* which she published in
1875. After leaving Lynn in a large respect due to the revolt
of most of her students,[18] Mrs. Eddy came to Boston and
opened what later became "The Massachusetts Metaphysical

---

[18]This point will be further discussed in Chapter II.

College" (571 Columbus Avenue) where she allegedly taught some 4,000 students at $300.00 per student for a period of eight years (1881-1889). One cannot help but wonder what would induce a reasonably-intelligent person to spend that amount of money for a course which never lasted the length of a college half-semester and which was taught by a staff hardly qualified intellectually to instruct the ninth grade. Mrs. Eddy herself knew comparatively nothing of Biblical history, theology, philosophy or the ancient languages. Christian Science sources have attempted for years to prove that Mrs. Eddy was a scholar in these fields, but the Rev. J. H. Wiggin, her literary adviser for some years, and himself an excellent scholar, has gone on record as saying that she was grossly ignorant of the subjects in question.

When Mrs. Eddy left the thankless community of Lynn, Massachusetts, she was then 61 years old and possessed less than 50 persons she could call "followers." As the calendar neared 1896, however, the indomitable will and perseverance of Mary Baker Eddy had begun to pay sizable dividends. Her churches and societies numbered well over 400 and the membership in them eventually increased from 800 to 900 per cent. Considering what she had to work with Mrs. Eddy accomplished a financial miracle and a propaganda goal unrivaled for its efficiency and ruthlessness.[19] From her ceaseless efforts for deification and wealth, there flowed continual revisions of *Science and Health*, which the "faithful" were commanded to purchase and sell, or stand in danger of excommunication from the Eddy Autocracy. Should the skeptical reader wish proof on this point of history, and Mrs. Eddy's insatiable greed for the comforts of financial security and power, we quote her announcement to that effect in its entirety:

> Christian Scientists in the United States and Canada are hereby enjoined not to teach a student of Christian Science for one year, commencing on March 14, 1897.

[19]See Chapter VII, *Christian Science Propaganda and Censorship.*

Miscellaneous Writings is calculated to prepare the minds of all true thinkers to understand the Christian Science textbook more correctly than a student can.

The Bible, *Science and Health, With Key to the Scriptures* and my other published works are the only proper instructors for this hour. It shall be the *duty* of all Christian Scientists to *circulate* and to *sell* as many of these books as they can.

If a member of the First Church of Christ, Scientist shall fail to *obey* this *injunction* it will render him liable to *lose* his *membership* in this church.—Mary Baker G. Eddy.*

Please pay close heed to what Mrs. Eddy said. She did not ask, she commanded all Scientists as their duty to her church to "circulate" and "sell" her works and "obey" her "injunction" under penalty of loss of membership. If, perchance, a method of blackmail is ever rendered legal, it could not be stated in more compelling terminology than this encyclical from the Eddy throne.

But let it be observed that her religious pandering was not limited to just one edition of *Science and Health* alone— no, Mrs. Eddy even extended her tactics to other fields. For example, in February, 1908, she "requested" all Christian Scientists to read the "new" edition of *Science and Health* which contained on page 442, beginning at line 30, information she affirmed to be of "great importance." Said Mrs. Eddy:

TAKE NOTICE

I request Christian Scientists universally to read the paragraph beginning at line 30 on page 442 in the edition of *Science and Health* which will be issued February 29. I consider the information there given to be of *great importance* at this state of the workings of Animal Magnetism, and it will *greatly aid* the students in their individual experiences.—Mary Baker G. Eddy.

One would assume from the tone of the language she used that here was a new revelation imperative to the defense against "Animal Magnetism" (the Fiend all Christian Scientists continually ward off mentally), but such was not the case;

Christian Science Journal, March, 1897.

instead Mrs. Eddy merely wrote what she had written a hundred times previously in different language. Said the material of "great importance":

> Christian Scientists, be a law to yourselves, that mental malpractice can harm you neither when asleep nor when awake.

Imagine $3.00 for these two sentences, the same old volume excepting this "new" sage advice, and countless loyal Scientists obliged her wish by dutifully pouring their gold pieces into the Eddy Treasury. It is no wonder that at her death Mrs. Eddy's personal fortune exceeded three million dollars. *None* of this, unfortunately, was left to charity.

Mrs. Eddy's reign had very little internal opposition and hence went unchallenged during her lifetime, but after her decease a definite scramble for control of her Empire ensued. All but the most exacting students of Christian Science history have overlooked this battle for the vacated throne of Christian Sciencedom, but it is an important historical conflict and one that deserves consideration. Upon the death of Mrs. Eddy the Christian Science Board of Directors, in good business fashion, assumed control of her thriving empire and consolidated this coup by obtaining from the Massachusetts Supreme Court authority for their self-perpetuating directorate. It was over this issue that a schism appeared in the ranks of Christian Science, and after assuming the title "The Christian Science Parent Church," under the leadership of Mrs. Annie C. Bill of London, the struggle commenced hot and heavy. John V. Dittemore, a member of the Christian Science Board of Directors, left the Boston camp and joined Mrs. Bill in editing the *Christian Science Watchman* and acclaimed her as Mrs. Eddy's successor. It was the contention of "The Parent Church" that Mrs. Eddy intended to have a successor within a half century of her demise and never intended a self-perpetuating Board of Directors. The directors, no doubt for good financial reasons, stoutly rejected this view and defended their new-found gold mine. On February 6, 1924, Mrs. Eddy's name was taken off *The Manual's* list of active officers and thus *The Watchman* claimed the Board had proven its original intentions by fully occupying the most powerful position in the Christian Science Church and forever eliminating the danger of a successor to Mrs. Eddy.[20] The claim by Mrs. Bill and Mr. Dittemore that the directors had usurped the authority of Mrs. Eddy and acted contrary to her expressed wishes went unchallenged for the most part by the Christian Science Board of Directors for Mr. Dittemore had strong evidence from *The Memoirs of Adam Dickey*, which the Board suppressed, and excerpts from the unpublished writings of Mrs. Eddy's secretary, Calvin A. Frye, that she expected a personal successor within fifty years. Wrote Mrs. Eddy:

> In answer to oncoming questions will say: I calculate that about one-half century more will bring to the front the man that God has equipped to lift aloft His standard of Christian Science (Vol. 4, No. 5, January, 1928).

It should also be noted that Mrs. Eddy herself said in a newspaper interview, May 1, 1901:

> No present change is contemplated in the rulership. You would ask, perhaps, whether my successor will be a woman or a man. I can answer that. It will be a man.
>
> Q. Can you name that man?
>
> A. I cannot answer that now.*

But as fate would have it, Mrs. Eddy never picked her successor, and with the advancing years the Christian Science Parent Church and *The Watchman* faded into obscurity and the controversy long since forgotten. However, it is a fact of history, nonetheless, that if by 1960 the Christian Science Church does not have a successor to Mrs. Eddy, then her prophecy will have become just another delusion of her old

---

[20]*The Christian Science Watchman*, Vol. 4, No. 7, March, 1928, pp. 153-154.

*The Christian Science Church maintains that she later amended this statement, saying that it referred to "generic man", or the human race, etc.

age, and the Christian Science Board of Directors will continue serenely their unchallenged reign.

As Mrs. Eddy neared the end of her long span (89 years) she ruled a "spiritual" corporation with regular magazines *(The Christian Science Journal* and *The Sentinel),* a newspaper *(The Christian Science Monitor),* and the hearts and souls of over 400,000 people who hailed her and her "discovery" as the saviours of their health.

Mary Baker Eddy died at her home in Chestnut Hill, Massachusetts, on December 3, 1910, of pneumonia and complications of old age, thus ending a life of the most remarkable character, progress and ingenuity seldom if ever observed in the annals of cultism. As her heritage Mrs. Eddy left a church over which she in the person of her book, *Science and Health,* is forever Pastor Emeritus, and this book the sole court of appeal in all disputes. The number of Christian Science practitioners, world-wide, as of January, 1955, was over 11,000, the membership of their churches exceeds 1,000,000,[21] there are 3,103 branches and 2,323 churches and societies, and the wealth of these enterprises supersedes even an over-generous estimate. One need look no further for evidence—Christian Science is marching on.

In drawing to a close this brief survey of Christian Science history, one can ill afford not to recognize the ever-growing power and prestige of Mrs. Eddy's philosophy. It has been wisely observed that the only good defense is a good offense. Let us not hesitate then as opponents of the most cherished principles of Christian Science to use every opportunity to refute them, for they are the teachings of probably the most remarkable and determined woman of the nineteenth century—Mary Baker Eddy.

---

[21]Figures on Christian Science membership are not generally advertised.

CHAPTER II

THE MYTH OF MOTHER EDDY

Many loyal Christian Scientists take great delight in stressing the saintly nature of Mary Baker Eddy, not to mention their assertion that she was the very personification of "boundless generosity." From the innumerable pages of the chief Christian Science periodicals through the years has come a gradual but definite legend about "Mother" Eddy,* until at last she has emerged a sainted old lady devoid of any attributes but those of incomparable perfection. Any criticism of her has met with tremendous opposition on the part of every known Christian Science pressure group, and the biographies of her life and works approved by the Christian Science organization abound with strenuous attempts to glorify her meager abilities. In truth one wonders, what with all the pro-Eddy propaganda promoted by her zealous disciples, how the truth about her has managed to be in evidence at all. But it does exist and despite the efforts of the Christian Science Church to suppress it, history tells a vivid but brutally candid tale of a grasping and jealous old woman who sold the heritage of her Christian birthright for a three-million-dollar fortune and the enduring adoration of her self-created church. The authors do not wish to appear bitter or one-sided where Mrs. Eddy is concerned, but must in sincerity judge her on the basis of all reliable evidence, which evidence, unfortunately, Christian Scientists in gen-

*Christian Scientists have quoted Mrs. Eddy to the effect that she never coveted this title (see Mark Twain, *Christian Science,* p. 331); however, in Section I, Article XXII of her own "By-Laws," Mrs. Eddy reserved the title for herself, exclusively, under threat of excommunication. She also addressed a personal telegram on May 27th, 1890, to the convention of the National Christian Science Association in New York City, which she signed "Mother Mary."

eral are not eager to have examined. It is also argued by
many sympathetic persons that since Mrs. Eddy has "passed
on" she should be allowed to rest in peace, "for after all,"
they say, "she really hasn't harmed anyone and her followers
are good Christians. Nothing can be gained by digging up
the past," they contend, "while much harm to the feelings of
Christian Scientists might be done." We must, however, take
exception to these objections for three principal reasons:
(1) The evil that men do often lives on after them, and the
evils of Mrs. Eddy and her system still live on after her,
and to all appearances are thriving world-wide. (2) There
is no conceivable Biblical ground upon which Christian
Science or its true followers may be called "Christian." Indeed the philosophy itself is the antithesis of the theology
of the entire New Testament. (3) Mrs. Eddy and Christian
Science, contrary to popular belief, have done much harm.
High on the list of their crimes is the common practice of
taking money for "curing" persons of diseases which their
own textbooks claim do not exist, allowing so-called practitioners whose abilities are nil (where properly diagnosed
organic diseases are in evidence) to peddle their untruthful
"treatments" to dying persons who will grasp at any straw,
and last but not least, the heinous crime of claiming that
Jesus Christ Himself is the center of this huge anti-Christian
business enterprise.

Christian Science is therefore a sect which cannot truth-
fully own the name "Christian," for in no sense imaginable
are they following the way of salvation so clearly preached
by the Son of God. The much talk about "love," "truth"
and "goodness" in Christian Science literature is far over-
shadowed by the fact that they and Mrs. Eddy have continually attacked almost every cardinal doctrine of the Christian faith by either denying it outright or by changing its
clear meaning into Mrs. Eddy's polyglot language.

Miss Georgine Milmine, who undertook the most thorough investigation of Mrs. Eddy's background ever attempted, and who has been attacked and vilified by Christian Scientists ever since, made a statement concerning her memorable work which stands as unchallenged today from a standpoint of evidence as when she made it. Said Miss Milmine upon hearing that Christian Scientists accused her book of saying only the "bad" things about Mrs. Eddy:

> I have searched the whole of Mrs. Eddy's life for a kindly, a generous, an unselfish, a fine womanly deed, and would have been only too glad to have recorded it, but have not found one.[1]

Doubtless, Christian Scientists universal will cite volumes of alleged kind and good works to defend Mrs. Eddy but it remains an uncontestable fact of history from those who knew her intimately and who were not hypnotized by her magnetic personality as were her devoted apologists, that Mrs. Eddy never did anything for anybody without a motive aimed at benefiting her own ends.

It is essential to understand the implications of Mrs. Eddy's teachings where religion in general and Christianity in particular are concerned, and one cannot but admire the dogmatic stand she took for what she alleged to be a "revelation." But be that as it may, it is also essential that the grounds for her belief and her practice of this "revelation" be equally understood. It has been wisely said that from the root springs the tree, and if the root be unsound the tree will be shaky and undependable. So then if Mrs. Eddy's principles and the practice of them are found to be unsound, it is only logical that the practice of those same principles by her followers should yield an equally unsound and shaky foundation for faith. It is this myth built up around Mrs.

---

[1]Georgine Milmine to F. W. Peabody as recorded in the latter's book, *The Religio-Medical Masquerade*, p. 73.

Eddy that has protected Christian Science from much powerful criticism which might otherwise have revealed the whole truth of her character and history. So then in the interest of a complete portrait of historical truth let us observe the real unvarnished Mrs. Eddy, her claims and her abilities, free of the adoration which colors the epic of her long and eventful life, and see if the legend of her person can endure the supreme court of final appeal—history. The authors leave the final conclusions with the interested reader who can judge for himself the value of this carefully erected legend which we have termed—The Myth of Mother Eddy.

The central claim of Mrs. Eddy and Christian Science is that she has "restored" to Christendom the power of healing "lost" since the days of the early church. It is continually reiterated in the literature of the cult that their "leader" healed as Jesus did and demonstrated through Divine Science. Not only this, but Mrs. Eddy herself boldly asserted that she healed all types of diseases including cancer, tuberculosis and diphtheria. Mrs. Eddy wrote to the *New York Sun,* December 19, 1898:

> I challenge the world to disprove what I hereby declare. After my discovery of Christian Science I healed consumption in the last stages that the M.D.'s by verdict of a stethoscope and the schools declared incurable, the lungs being mostly consumed. I healed malignant tubercular diphtheria and carious bones that could be dented by the finger, saving them when the surgeon's instruments were lying on the table ready for their amputation. I have healed at one visit a cancer that had so eaten the flesh of the neck as to expose the jugular vein so that it stood out like a cord.

Notice here Mrs. Eddy gives no particulars, names of patients, localities, dates or witnesses. Indeed the only persons who ever witnessed her "miraculous" cures were either hypnotized lackeys of Mrs. Eddy's without medical training to justify their diagnosis of disease, or Christian Scientists of another era who unfortunately believe as God-breathed truth

any claim that either Mrs. Eddy or her contemporary wor-
shipers have conjured up. And so this key phase of the Eddy
myth—Mrs. Eddy's power to heal—presents itself as a unique
challenge. For if it be true that she healed with such power,
then Mrs. Eddy stands vindicated of any evil. If it is false,
she is unmasked as a deceiver of unparalleled cruelty, preying
upon the sick and maimed for personal remuneration, prestige
and cheap sensational publicity. Briefly then, let us consider
this phase of "Mother" Eddy's[2] long career.

To begin with, it should be realized in the process of in-
vestigating Mrs. Eddy's healing claims that she refused outright to treat identical cases of diseases she claimed to have
cured. Even when a prominent Cincinnati physician offered
her every such opportunity, Mrs. Eddy remained strangely
silent; indeed she never mentioned the issue again.[3] This is
hardly the attitude one would expect from the alleged "successor to Jesus Christ." The foregoing is only one fact of a
large number, which prove beyond doubt that Mrs. Eddy
did not heal as she claimed. During her long life Mrs. Eddy
allowed her own little granddaughter, her beloved brother
Samuel's wife, and her close friend, Joseph Armstrong, all
to die painful deaths of cancer, pneumonia and pleurisy, and
never to any known evidence of the contrary did she ever lift
her "healing" hand to save them.[4] Instead she recommended
"absent treatment" in all three cases which consisted of
reading her book, *Science and Health,* and concentrating
upon mentally repulsing the organic deterioration. Mrs.
Eddy could have at least paid a call on them, and if her
claims were true, healed them "at one visit," but she did not

[2]A self-conferred title of Mrs. Eddy; see the *Christian Science Sentinel,* December 21, 1899.

[3]*New York Sun,* January 1, 1899, by Dr. Charles A. L. Reed.

[4]She did, however, send her personal check to defray the cost of her sister-in-law's operation, but by the time the surgeon operated, the time taken in useless Christian Science treatments had taken a fatal toll and she died.

because she could not, and no one knew it better than Mary
Baker Eddy. There is an overwhelming mass of evidence
from sources unchallengeable that this fact is absolute truth,
and no better authority can be quoted than the sworn testimony of Mr. Alfred Farlow, then chairman of the Publications Committee of the Christian Science Church and President of the Mother Church in Boston. Mr. Farlow's testimony,
that of a Christian Scientist in excellent standing with his
church and certainly in a position to know the facts about
Mrs. Eddy, clearly stated that he did not know of *any*
healing *ever* having been made by Mrs. Eddy of *any* organic
disease in her entire life but that of stiff leg—hardly a major
illness by any reasonable diagnosis. (*The Religio-Medical Masquerade*, F. W. Peabody, p. 113.) Much more material
could be introduced to further verify this contention of history
against the Eddy healing legend, but it is sufficient to say
that the issue needs no further support. She who professed
to "succeed Jesus Christ" as the great healer of our age
could not even heal her closest emotional contacts, and to
conceal this great threat to her system which was based
squarely on her alleged power to heal, Mrs. Eddy and her
contemporaries have masqueraded to the world and to her
gullible followers the legend of her miraculous curative power.
This power, so widely trumpeted by Christian Science propaganda, history tells us she never exercised or demonstrated
openly for the obvious reason that it was a complete illusion,
a phantom of Christian Science publicity and the delusions
of Mary Baker Eddy. However, we shall proceed with the
investigation of the other facets of the Eddy myth.

In 1932 there appeared a work so devastating in its documentary evidence, and so unimpeachable in its source that
Christian Scientists today do not even care to admit its
existence. We refer to the book, *Mary Baker Eddy, The Truth
and the Tradition*, by Ernest Sutherland Bates and John V.

Dittemore. Mr. Dittemore,* a former luminary in the Eddy
hierarchy, headed up the Christian Science publication committee in New York (1908), was a director of the Mother
Church in Boston (1909-1919), and a trustee under the will
of Mary Baker Eddy (1910-1920). The material upon which the
book was based constituted literally two trunks full of copies
of Mrs. Eddy's letters (over 2,000 of them), photostatic reproductions of her poems, scrapbooks and her unpublished com-
mentary on the Scriptures. This, along with other suppressed
material, was taken from the very files of the Christian Science
Church. It defies contradiction. For the benefit of any curious
skeptic who doubts Mr. Dittemore's devotion when a leading
Christian Scientist, let it be remembered that he personally
financed Sibyl Wilbur's biography of Mrs. Eddy published
in 1907, which has the official approval of the Christian
Science Church. In this connection it is interesting to note
what one who knew all the facts has to say about that
"biography." Mr. Dittemore wrote: "The contents of that
volume were mostly provided for the author from *Church
sources* and in the light of subsequent knowledge, have largely
proved *unreliable*."[5] Mr. Dittemore's belief that the whole
history about Mrs. Eddy and Christian Science should be told
led him to author this book with Dr. Bates, and it was written
mainly to offset what the authors also vigorously contend—
namely, that Mrs. Eddy's true life story has been cleverly
supplanted by a manufactured history, a gross perversion of
facts and truth. Mr. Dittemore stated:

A few years after Mrs. Eddy's decease, however, the newer
elements (in the Christian Science hierarchy) sought to dissuade me

---

*Mr. Dittemore, as previously mentioned, left the Christian Science Church after
Mrs. Eddy's death, as a result of the controversy over Mrs. Bill's claim to leadership; he later sent a letter to the Church in which he apologized for his criticism
of Mrs. Eddy and hailed her as a great healer and leader. However, Mr. Dittemore never repudiated his charge that the Christian Science Church was con-
structing a legend around Mrs. Eddy's memory; indeed, history has verified his
claims; therefore, any objections by Christian Scientists to the validity of Mr.
Dittemore's statements are completely groundless and irrelevant.

[5]*Mary Baker Eddy, The Truth and the Tradition,* Preface III.

from my purpose as facts unfolded relating to matters in her history certain to interfere with what had become the unacknowledged, but nonetheless actual, determination *to create a legendary Mrs. Eddy.* The recent Powell[6] biography is the sign and symbol of that official determination, supported by the present strange psychology of the membership.[7]

What could be more conclusive than this crystal clear statement? Mr. Dittemore as a high, though honest, Christian Science official, saw the Eddy legend evolving from intimate personal contact with the subject in question. Who with a fair mind can deny his book or its judgments?

"But what of Mrs. Eddy's generosity and kindness?" say gullible Christian Scientists and their sympathizers. "Surely a woman of such traits could not traffic in human health for mere monetary gain?"

To this the authors answer not only could she, but she did so openly, and without remorse. It will be recalled that the Lord Jesus Christ said during His ministry when speaking of the gifts of God:

"Heal the sick, cleanse the lepers, raise the dead, cast out devils: *freely* ye have received, *freely* give" (Matt. 10:8).

But this was not the attitude of Mrs. Eddy who alleges she follows in the footsteps of Jesus, nor has it been the apparent attitude of Christian Science practitioners in general practice. Wrote Mrs. Eddy concerning the treatments of Christian Science:

Christian Science demonstrates that the patient who *pays* whatever he is able to pay for *healing* is more apt to recover than he who withholds the slight equivalent for health.[*]

It is easily seen by this that Christian Science definitely endorses "pay as you go" healing. Indeed, prompt cash in large amounts seemed to make one "more apt to recover than he who withholds the slight equivalent for health." The thoughtful reader is left to interpret this dollar-and-cents healing as

---

[6]*Mary Baker Eddy,* by Lyman P. Powell.
[7]*Mary Baker Eddy, The Truth and the Tradition,* Preface IV.
[*]Riley, Peabody & Humiston, *The Faith, Falsity and Failure of Christian Science,* p. 267, Fleming Revel, 1926.

best as he can in relation to the plain declaration by our Lord that it should be "freely given." Mrs. Eddy was also not above acting as "agent" for her ardent pupils, for the customary ten per cent commission, of course, and in 1870, when first embarking upon her "healing" career, she drew up a contract with said pupils which rivals any of our contemporary theatrical or "loan shark" agreements for its financial stranglehold. The contract of the "generous" Mrs. Glover stipulated as follows:

We, the undersigned, do hereby agree in consideration of instruction [twelve weeks] and a manuscript [Quimby's] received from Mrs. Mary B. Glover, to pay her $100.00 *in advance* and 10% annually on the income that we receive from practicing or teaching the same. We also do hereby agree to pay the said Mary B. Glover $1,000.00 in case we do not practice or teach the same she has taught us.[8]

Signed—D. A. Spofford
M. A. Spofford

As Shakespeare so graphically portrayed it, Shylock must have his pound of flesh, and Mrs. Eddy even went to court to get it. She never won any of the suits, however, since no judge ever thought her lessons worth that much, or her claims even worthy of serious consideration.

Continuing further into the Eddy legend, we are once again confronted with the cold, impartial testimony of history where Mrs. Eddy's boundless "generosity" and "selflessness" are concerned. Shortly after the famous "Woodbury Suit" wherein Mrs. Eddy was accused of slandering a former disciple, the Christian Science treasury showed a marked decrease in volume, the result of large legal fees due in consideration of services rendered during the case. As a result of this, Mrs. Eddy perpetrated on the "faithful" the infamous "Teajacket swindle" calculated to draw from her gullible followers the revenue with which to further strengthen her treasury. In line with this scheme she drafted the follow-

[8]*Ibid*, p. 267.

ing "request" to her Church universal which appeared in the *Christian Science Journal*, December 21, 1899:

> Beloved, I ask this favor of all Christian Scientists. Do not give me on, before, or after the forthcoming holiday aught material except three tea-jackets. *All may contribute to these.* One learns to value material things only as one needs them, and the costliest things are the ones that one needs most. Among my present needs material are these—three jackets, two of darkish, heavy silk, the shade appropriate to white hair; the third of heavy satin, lighter shade, but sufficiently sombre. Nos. 1 and 2 to be common-sense jackets for Mother to work in, and not over-trimmed by any means. No. 3 for best, such as she can afford for her dressing room.—Mary Baker Eddy.

The key to this whole financial angle is to be found in five short words, "*All may contribute to these.*" Notice Mrs. Eddy does not request two hundred thousand teajackets,[9] merely "contributions" toward them. No one was to send them—only send the money to buy them. "Mother" Eddy must have enjoyed this neat trick of replenishing her gold reserve, and none can deny that it was carried off with a finesse that rivals any confidence game ever conceived. All this, mind you, in the name of Jesus Christ and under the banner of Christian Science, allegedly the true religion. Judge Rutherford of Jehovah's Witnesses could not have had Christian Science too far out of mind when he said, "Religion is a racket." Compared to Mrs. Eddy, "Pastor" Russell and Judge Rutherford of The Watch Tower were rank amateurs at collecting money. She played for the highest stakes at all times, and with Mary Baker Eddy it was always "winner take all," and she did!

The reader may wonder at this point, "Certainly Mrs. Eddy never hoped to practice such things indefinitely; even she must have known someone would eventually expose her, didn't she?" The answer to this common question is to be found in Mrs. Eddy's further financial exploits. Instead of being satisfied with her "gold harvest," the mistress of

---

[9]Estimated Christian Science Church membership in 1899.

Pleasant View and Chestnut Hill[10] soon followed it up with a second financial coup, a truly masterful fund-raising campaign, even less subtle than the "teajacket" fiasco. Wrote Mrs. Eddy in the February issue of the *Christian Science Journal,* February 18, 1909:

> *Christian Science Spoons*—On each of these most beautiful spoons is a motto in bas-relief that every person on earth needs to hold in thought. Mother *"requests"*[11] that Christian Scientists shall not ask to be informed what this motto is but each Scientist shall purchase at least one spoon, and those that can afford it, one dozen spoons, that their family may read this motto at every meal, and their guests be made partakers of its simple truth.—Mary Baker G. Eddy.

The reader can form his own opinions on this episode in Mrs. Eddy's career as a promoter, but let him do so with all the facts in mind. The spoons sold for $3.00 and $5.00 respectively (silver and gold), and engraved upon them was this earth-shaking inscription from the pen of "Mother" Eddy, *"Not matter, but mind satisfieth."* Think of it! On a spoon which feeds the body they deny exists, Mrs. Eddy made financial idiots of her entire church.* Who can deny that instead of "boundless generosity," it was indeed immeasurable greed that fired the furnace of her literary ambitions and helped establish the myth of "Mother" Eddy? One need hardly multiply the fantastic profits derived from this scheme. But allowing that the spoons cost half their selling price, she still realized over a quarter of a million dollars profit, and it was given willingly. As Mark Twain once said with his inimitable wit: "The human race delights in making

---

[10] Two of her palatial dwelling places.

[11] The emphasis is the authors'.

* It has been maintained by the Christian Science Church that neither Mrs. Eddy nor her Church ever had any interest in the company that manufactured the spoons, hence no profit was derived from the transaction. We, of course, never said that Mrs. Eddy or the Church was interested in the company; we only maintain that they profited either jointly or separately from the sale of the spoons, probably on a contract or percentage basis. And if the Christian Science Church is willing to make their financial records of this period available for observation, we shall be happy to retract the statement—but until then the evidence still points toward a profit-making venture and will continue to be treated as such.

asininity a career." Where Mrs. Eddy's followers are concerned we must heartily concur, for who but deluded mortals
would deny the reality of the food they eat and the diseases
they are dying from, not to mention the very Deity of the
Lord that bought them with His own blood. These things
Mrs. Eddy and all her followers have never ceased to do
despite the fact that hospitals and cemeteries the world over
abound with ample testimony that sickness, suffering and
death are *real,* and not to be dismissed as Christian Scientists
dismiss them, with meaningless words and the treatments
of useless* "quack" practitioners. The complete story of
Mrs. Eddy may never be fully known before the day of judgment, but it is in evidence for all to see that the legend of
her person and power is directly in contradiction to all that
history reveals, and truth will allow. This chapter is therefore
only one more earnest plea for a closer look at, and evaluation
of, this amazing woman—Mary Baker Eddy—of whom it has
been truly written that in her, history clearly reveals "how
a woman becomes a deity."

---

*Where medically verified diagnosis of organic disease is concerned.

CHAPTER III

CHRISTIAN SCIENCE VS. THE QUIMBY MANUSCRIPTS

Phineas Parkhurst Quimby, whose pupil Mrs. Eddy was from 1862 to 1864, has been the proverbial skeleton in the Christian Science closet for seventy-eight years, and the bones are still rattling—"for he being dead yet speaketh." The illustrious "Dr." (by courtesy only) Quimby has been maligned almost as much as Frederick W. Peabody, the great nemesis of Mrs. Eddy, and numerous chapters in Christian Science literature have been devoted to proving that "there is nothing worthy of the name manuscripts in the Quimby safe."[1] Indeed, leading Christian Science apologists have gone to great lengths to prove that Mrs. Eddy left *her* manuscripts with Quimby and "unselfishly" affixed *his* name to *her* writings. They have carefully constructed what is probably the greatest deliberate falsehood ever perpetrated upon the literary world and their deluded fellow Scientists, one truly worthy of the name hoax. In brief, knowing the Quimby Manuscripts exist (they are in the vault of the Library of Congress), and that Mrs. Eddy had access to at least one of them and even copied and taught its contents as Quimby's, not hers (1867-1870), they have masqueraded to the world that it is a legend, "The Quimby Manuscript Tradition," as Miss Wilbur blatantly states it.[2]

Recently in Norman Beasley's book (*The Cross and the Crown*—the History of Christian Science), a syrupy one-sided and biased historical apology for Mrs. Eddy and her religion, the false Quimby Manuscript idea is unconcernedly

---

[1] *The Life of Mary Baker Eddy*, Sibyl Wilbur, p. 99.
[2] *Ibid*, p. 101.

overlooked. Writes Mr. Beasley without a blush, and against all historical evidence:

There is a familiarity in some of the so-called "Quimby Manuscripts" to her writings, but examination of all of Mrs. Eddy's writings and all of Quimby's writings *will dismiss doubt and erase speculation over their authorship.* . . . To accept the claim that Mrs. Eddy obtained her science of healing from Quimby *is to reject all the words and works of the great Teacher.* Nothing could be more separated from the truth than such an allegation. Mrs. Eddy did not obtain her high affirmation of God from Quimby. *She obtained it by going to the Bible and listening. The great servants in the Kingdom of the Spirit have always done that—listened.*[3]

The reader will note that for Mr. Beasley to challenge Mrs. Eddy's source of "revelation," and even consider Quimby, "is to reject all the words and works of the great Teacher." Obviously Jesus Christ is here meant and it is specifically inferred, if not expressly declared, that Mrs. Eddy is a true disciple of His in every sense of the word. It is rather apparent, as his scant index reveals, that Mr. Beasley has not considered seriously any sources but those favorable to Mrs. Eddy and her church.[4] The flyleaf of his book says, "[This][5] history, which has been in preparation for twenty years, is also a work of the most careful scholarship and *interpretation.*" In the light of Mr. Beasley's "history," the authors agree wholeheartedly with the last word here quoted, for in many places it is not a true record in any sense of history, but a markedly pro-Christian Science "interpretation" of history. Mr. Beasley attempts the role of a theologian when he declares that Mrs. Eddy obtained "her high affirmation of God . . . by going to the Bible and listening." Unfortunately for the role he attempts, Mr. Beasley is ill-prepared and grossly misinformed, for no theologian who has ever lived in the annals of Judaism

---

[3] (New York, Little, Brown & Co.) pp. 149-150.
[4] One of the many historical perversions in Mr. Beasley's book is the affirmation that Mrs. Eddy was miraculously healed after a fall on the ice in Lynn, Massachusetts, 1866, and thus discovered Christian Science. This account, as has been shown, is a complete falsehood and proof that Mr. Beasley is a poor historian.
[5] The brackets are ours.

or Christianity (which faiths Mrs. Eddy professes to base her theology on), has ever entertained her garbled and un-Biblical concept of the Deity. The God of the Bible is a Personality, but the god of Christian Science is an "It," devoid of personality and reduced to a mere Principle. Contrary to Mr. Beasley's pronounced historical ramblings, the Bible clearly testifies that Mrs. Eddy got none of her metaphysical hallucinations from it; she merely borrowed Biblical terminology wherever it suited her purposes and merrily rejected whatever contradicted her philosophy. The authors are prepared to prove this with material far too exhaustive to quote here.[6] Let it be thoroughly understood that Mrs. Eddy, from the standpoint of historical Christian theology, was no "great servant in the kingdom of the spirit," as Mr. Beasley represents her. Rather, she ranks as one of the great and pitiful tragedies of Christendom whose religion has lured many down "the broad way which leadeth unto destruction" and spiritual death. But be that as it may, the Quimby Manuscripts still loom ominously on the historical scene vigorously contesting the artificial history of Christian Science architects and their supporters. The official position of Mrs. Eddy, and consequently all Christian Scientists, from the beginning of the Quimby-Eddy controversy, has been that Mrs. Eddy left her manuscripts with Quimby and that she, not he, is the author of the Christian Science philosophy. Sibyl Wilbur, chief apologist for the Eddy Legend, has written—"It has been shown that Mrs. Patterson in 1862 wrote certain manuscripts for Quimby and gave them to him."[7] This declaration by Miss Wilbur in the light of history is of course a complete falsehood, and no better authority can be cited than George A. Quimby who was for years his father's private secretary, clerk, bookkeeper and intimate confidante. Said Mr. Quimby in answer to the fraudulent claims of Mrs. Eddy and Miss

[6]This subject is further treated in Chapter IV.
[7]*Life of Mary Baker Eddy*, p. 96.

Wilbur: "She (Mrs. Eddy) heard many of his essays read; wrote many herself which she submitted to him for inspection and correction. *But she never left any of hers with him.* She gave him full credit for curing her and teaching her the very ideas she later had revealed to her from heaven."[8] Christian Science propaganda has cleverly omitted any comment on this issue preferring to publish only Mrs. Eddy's side of the question; but, contrary to both the Christian Science Church and Mr. Beasley, who hold that "examination of all of Mrs. Eddy's writings and all of Quimby's writings will dismiss doubt and erase speculation over their authorship,"[9] it is a proven fact that there are approximately two thousand references[10] in the Quimby Manuscripts, which can be readily recognized by both Christian Scientists and non-Scientists, as having their parallels in Mrs. Eddy's writings. It is not a question of opinion, as Christian Scientists would like to leave it, but a matter of cold dispassionate fact. Quimby did not write *Science and Health,* on this all agree, but without him it never could have come into existence for he was its father as surely as Mrs. Eddy was its mother. The Christian Science Church, however, has endlessly parroted Mrs. Eddy who claimed that her authorship and title, "Discoverer and Founder of Christian Science," were vindicated by the courts of our country. Christian Scientists sit smugly behind this hollow assertion, owning that Mrs. Eddy is "legally" the author of Christian Science, but true to form they conveniently neglect to tell the whole story of the case in question, since it decidedly refutes their contentions.

In February of 1883 Mr. E. J. Arens published certain material from Mrs. Eddy's copyrighted books which he declared were in reality the teachings of P. P. Quimby, not Mrs. Eddy, and thus did not need her sanction. Arens was promptly

[8]*The Quimby Manuscripts,* edition of 1921, Horatio Dresser, editor, pp. 436-437.
[9]*The Cross and the Crown,* p. 150.
[10]*Mary Baker Eddy's Early Writings Compared With the Quimby Manuscripts* by Jeane Philips, p. 7.

sued by the ever-vigilant queen of Christian Science who arose
to the defense of her throne and charged violation of copyright. George A. Quimby, however, refused to allow his
father's Manuscripts to be shown in court; hence Arens lost
the case and Mrs. Eddy's copyright was assured validity.
From this litigation Mrs. Eddy and the Christian Science
Church drew two entirely unwarranted assumptions: (1)
The erroneous idea that because the Quimby Manuscripts
were not shown at the trial, therefore they did not exist. (2)
The verdict in favor of Mrs. Eddy establishes her as the
originator of Christian Science and not Quimby. Thus in
the words of Horatio Dresser, "The rumor is persistently
fostered that the whole question of Mrs. Eddy's indebtedness
was settled by the Arens suit."[11] In view of these two utterly
fallacious assumptions candor dictates that they be quickly
repudiated and the record set aright.

First, let it be understood from a legal standpoint that
Mrs. Eddy's victory only established one fact—namely that
she was the legal owner of the copyright to *Science and
Health*—nothing more! Second, the question of Quimby's
authorship could not be decided without the Quimby Manuscripts, and these George Quimby was not willing to allow
Arens the use of—but which were finally published in 1921,
which publication completely demolished the Christian Science
arguments. Proof that the Quimby Manuscripts were detrimental to Christian Science claims is the fact that the first
edition was mysteriously bought up and copies of the second
edition are at this date almost impossible to obtain. Books
harmful to Christian Science or Mrs. Eddy usually travel
this rapid route to oblivion as evidenced by the unusual dis-
appearance of Georgine Milmine's "Life" of Mrs. Eddy and
Adam Dickey's *Memoirs of Mary Baker Eddy*, both of which
are now virtually unobtainable. Following their defeat along

[11]*The Quimby Manuscripts*, p. 435.

this line of evidence where the Quimby Manuscripts were concerned, the successors to Mrs. Eddy took up a second line of defense claiming that she unselfishly offered to have the Quimby Manuscripts published at her own expense so as to end the "false" rumors about their bearing on her "discovery." Sibyl Wilbur sarcastically infers in her biography of Mrs. Eddy that George Quimby's failure to respond to Mrs. Eddy's invitation proves that no manuscripts existed. But Miss Wilbur again states only half the case. The authors have taken the liberty of reproducing Mrs. Eddy's "fair offer" to George A. Quimby. Note, please, the entire proposition in her own words:

Mr. George A. Quimby, son of the late Phineas P. Quimby—over his own signature, and before a witness—stated, in 1883, that he had in his possession at that time *all* the manuscripts written by his father. I hereby declare to expose the falsehood of parties publicly intimating that I have appropriated matter belonging to the aforesaid Quimby, that I will pay the cost of printing and publishing the first edition of these manuscripts, with the author's name attached:

Provided—that I am allowed first to examine such manuscripts, and that I find they were Mr. P. P. Quimby's own compositions, and not mine, that were left with him many years ago—or that they have not since his death, in 1865, been stolen from my published works; and also, that I am given the right to bring out this one edition under copyright of said owner of said manuscripts, and that all the money accruing from the sale of the book shall be paid to said owner. Some of Mr. Quimby's purported writings, quoted by J. A. Dresser, were my own words, as nearly as I can recall them.

There is a great demand for my book, *Science and Health*. Hence Mr. Dresser's excuse for the delay in publishing Quimby's manuscripts, namely, that this age is not sufficiently enlightened to be benefited by them [?] is lost; for if I have copied from Quimby, and my book is accepted, this acceptance creates a demand for his writings.[12]

The reader will observe that Mrs. Eddy wanted to *examine* the Manuscripts to see if they were *hers* which she alleged she left with Quimby. In brief, she wanted the prerogative of censoring what she knew to be Quimby's Manuscripts, because she taught from a copy of them in

[12]*Christian Science Journal*, June, 1887.

Stoughton, Massachusetts (1867-1870). In answer to her
empty offer, George A. Quimby wrote:

> Just think of it! My letting her or anyone else have Manuscripts
> *I knew* were Father's because *I saw* him write them, and copied many
> of them myself to see if *she* didn't write them and leave them with him.
> The religion which she teaches certainly is hers, for which I cannot be
> too thankful; and I should be loath to go down to my grave feeling that
> my Father was in any way connected with Christian Science. That she
> got her inspiration and ideas from Father is beyond question.[13]

Breathing closely on the neck of Mrs. Eddy's tottering
claims to Christian Science "discovery," the candidly reliable
New York Times published in 1904 a devastating critique of
Mrs. Eddy's religion and theology which shattered all Christian Science efforts to let the issue rest without further controversy. Said the *Times*:

> Evidence has come into the possession of the *New York Times* which
> throws a flood of light on the hitherto more or less mysterious origin of
> Christian Science and reveals exactly what that origin was. This evidence
> proves what hitherto has only been suspected, that Mrs. Mary Baker
> Eddy's present version of its origin, the only one she has given or
> admitted for many years, is absolutely false, that her system of healing
> was not as she asserts—revealed to her by God in the year 1866—but
> that at least for four years after that time she not only admitted but
> proclaimed that it was revealed to her by Phineas Parkhurst Quimby
> of Portland, Maine, and that neither she nor Quimby had at any time
> ever made any claims of divine revelation.

Taking advantage of this firsthand evidence, a copy of
Quimby's Manuscripts from which Mrs. Eddy taught (1867-
1870) and which was emended in Mrs. Eddy's own handwriting, the *Times* literally tore to pieces her false pretenses
and delusions and clearly traced Christian Science to Quimby,
all her propaganda notwithstanding. The results were disas-
trous for Mrs. Eddy's carefully-manufactured "history" of the
Christian Science movement, and she was compelled to sum-
mon all her forces to meet the new challenge. Consequently
a flood of literature by Sibyl Wilbur, Septimus J. Hanna, R. C.

---

[13]*The Quimby Manuscripts*, pp. 436-438.

Douglass, Lyman Powell and numerous Christian Science sympathizers attempted to offset this damning evidence in one way or another. Miss Wilbur, a reporter with financial visions of security, manufactured the "Quimby Manuscript tradition" idea and not until 1921, the date of the publication of the disputed manuscripts, was this unprincipled hoax unmasked. Miss Wilbur knew full well that the Quimby Manuscripts existed, in fact she saw exact copies of what are now safely filed in the Library of Congress. In a statement to the *New York World,* May, 1907, and in answer to Sibyl Wilbur's contention that his father's Manuscripts did not exist, George Quimby wrote:

. . . If the fair or rather the unfair Sibyl can make herself or anybody else believe that I do not possess them, after having seen them herself, why I shall have to bear the cross as best I can and go down to the grave with the knowledge that Father did not write the Manuscripts which I know he did write because I saw him do it. Sibyl says he didn't, and of course she ought to know because she knows nothing about it anyhow. The above statement is what is called logic, and it is useless to butt your head against it.

The writings I possess now belong to me. They have either been in the possession of Father or myself since some years before Mrs. Eddy ever saw Father; therefore I find it awfully hard to make myself really believe that they are the Manuscripts Mrs. Eddy left with him—when as a matter of fact she never left any—or that she gave him the ideas contained in the Manuscripts several years before they ever saw each other, or that she ever had such ideas.

I have never paraded these ideas before the public. I have elected, so far, not to publish them. I have allowed parties to examine them under certain restrictions, as I have a perfect right to do. I allowed Sibyl the same privilege and she is the first person in forty years to doubt their authenticity. And she only doubted with her pen—for she knew they were just what I told her they were and that they were authentic when she made her pen say they were not; and I'll bet her pen turned red in the face when it expressed that doubt.

This letter of George Quimby's only serves to add one more concrete testimonial to the already tremendous file which incontestably proves that Mrs. Eddy and her followers have no desire whatever to tell the *real* truth about her or her religion. For to tell the whole truth about so explosive an issue would be to invite disaster, and damage, if not destruction, to the myth of her successorship to Jesus Christ—a cherished Christian Science illusion.

Mark Twain in his blistering exposé of Mrs. Eddy and her cult[14] made the following statement concerning the Quimby-Eddy controversy:

> All the world and God added could not convince a Scientist (intelligent or otherwise) that Mrs. Eddy's claim to the authorship is a lie and a swindle.[15]

The incomparable Mr. Twain went even further than George Quimby in his assertion based on a literary evaluation of Mrs. Eddy's book. But even he was destined to suffer betrayal at the hands of a "loyal" confidante, one Albert B. Paine, an alleged recipient of Christian Science "cures" and himself kindly disposed toward Mrs. Eddy's camp. This biographer of Twain conveniently waited until the great humorist was safely buried and his anti-Eddy campaigns in a dormant state, and then boldly represented him as having negated all he ever said of a critical nature about Mrs. Eddy by elevating her to a place in the Trinity of God. Said Mark Twain, allegedly speaking to Paine and according to Paine's biography:

> Of course you have benefited. Christian Science is humanity's boon. Mother Eddy deserves a place in the Trinity as much as any member of it. She has organized and made available a healing principle that for two thousand years has never been employed except as the merest guesswork. She is the benefactor of the age.*

By way of showing what Mark Twain's *true* attitude toward Mrs. Eddy and Christian Science was, the authors here quote one of his pointed appraisals of her, and one which he never altered, in either his books or lectures.

> Mrs. Eddy. . . grasping, sordid, penurious, famishing for everything she sees—money, power, glory—vain, untruthful, jealous, despotic, arro-

---

[14]*Christian Science*, Mark Twain.
[15]Mark Twain's personal letter, New York, April 17, 1903.
*Albert B. Paine, *Mark Twain, A Biography*, 1923, Harper & Brothers.

gant, insolent, pitiless where thinkers and hypnotists are concerned, illiterate, shallow, incapable of reasoning outside of commercial lines, immeasurably selfish—.[16]

If one can read the works of Mark Twain on Mrs. Eddy and her religion, and then read what this "accurate" pro-Christian Science biographer says he said, and still believe for one moment that Mr. Twain ever uttered such blasphemous nonsense, then the mental processes of our age stand in grave psychological jeopardy. There is no limit, as this example shows, as to how far Christian Scientists and their sympathizers have gone, both to deify Mrs. Eddy[17] and to defend her precepts. To them she was the modern counterpart of Jesus Christ and they have not hesitated to make the comparison.

This is indeed an amazing picture of progress unrivaled in the history of cultism. From P. P. Quimby's humble office in Portland to the regal splendor of Chestnut Hill and the Mother Church in Boston, Mary Baker Eddy ascended the throne of Christian Science with a scepter of absolute power, which only the angel of death was able to wrest from her palsied hand. She was master until the end and even Quimby's Manuscripts could never deprive her of the acclaim and adoration of her peculiar creation, the Christian Science Church.

Solely for the purpose of documenting the Quimby-Eddy controversy beyond a shadow of doubt, the authors have taken the liberty of listing in parallel columns some of the teachings of Mrs. Eddy as compared to those of the Quimby Manuscripts which we are prepared to supplement with photostatic copies of the same Manuscripts containing Mrs. Eddy's corrections in her own handwriting. The following data is taken from "Dr." Quimby's Manuscript, *Questions and Answers,* which antedates Mrs. Eddy's "discovery" of Christian Science by a considerable number of years:

---

[16]*Christian Science,* Mark Twain, 1907, p. 285.
[17]*Mary Baker Eddy,* by Ernest S. Bates and J. V. Dittemore, p. 311.

From Quimby's *Science of Man,* expounded by Mrs. Eddy at Stoughton, 1868, 1869, 1870.

From Mrs. Eddy's *Science and Health,* the textbook of the "Christian Science" she now claims to have discovered in 1866.

If I understand how disease originates in the mind and fully believe it, why cannot I cure myself?

Disease being made by our belief or by our parents' belief or by public opinion there is no formula of argument to be adopted, but every one must fit in their particular case. There it requires great shrewdness or wisdom to get the better of the error. . .

I know of no better counsel than Jesus gave to his disciples when he sent them forth to cast out devils and heal the sick, and thus in practice to preach the Truth, "Be ye wise as serpents and harmless as doves." Never get into a passion, but in patience possess ye your soul, and at length you weary out the discord and produce harmony by your Truth destroying error. Then you get the case. Now, if you are not afraid to face the error and argue it down, then you can heal the sick.

The patient's disease is in his belief.

Error is sickness. Truth is health.

In this science the names are given; thus God is Wisdom. This Wisdom, not an Individuality but a principle every idea—form, of which the idea, man, is the highest —hence the image of God, or the Principle.

Disease being a belief, a latent delusion of mortal mind, the sensation would not appear if *this error was met and destroyed by Truth.*—page 61, edition of 1898.

Science not only reveals the origin of all disease as wholly mental, but it also declares that all disease is cured by mind.—page 62—edition of 1898.

When we come to have more faith in the Truth of Being than we have in error, more faith in spirit than in matter, then no material conditions can prevent us from healing the sick, *and destroying error through Truth.*—page 367—edition of 1898.

We classify disease as error which nothing but Truth or Mind can heal.—page 427, edition of 1898.

Discord is the nothingness of error. Harmony is the somethingness of Truth.—page 172—edition of 1898.

Sickness is part of the error which Truth casts out.—page 478—edition of 1898.

God is the principle of man; and the principle of man remaining perfect, its idea or reflection—man remains perfect.—page 466—edition of 1898.

Man was and is God's idea.—page 231—edition of 1898.

Man is the idea of Divine Principle.—page 471—edition of 1898.

What is God? Jehovah is not a

person. God is Principle.—page 169
—edition of 1881.

Understanding is God.
All sciences are part of God.
Truth is God.
There is no other Truth but God.
God is Wisdom.
God is Principle.

Wisdom, Love, Truth are the
Principle.

Understanding is a quality of
God.—page 449—edition of 1898.
All Science is of God.—page 513,
edition of 1898.

Truth is God.—page 183—edition
of 1898.
Truth, God, is not the Father
of error.—page 469, edition of
1898.
How can I most rapidly advance
in the understanding of Christian
Science? Study thoroughly the
letter and imbibe the spirit. Adhere to its divine Principle, and
follow its behests, abiding steadily
in Wisdom, Love and Truth.—page
491, edition of 1898.

Error is matter.
Matter has no intelligence.
To give intelligence to matter is
an error which is sickness.

Matter has no intelligence of its
own, and to believe intelligence is
in matter is the error which produced pain and inharmony of all
sorts; to hold ourselves we are a
principle outside of matter, we
would not be influenced by the
opinions of man, but held to the
workings only of a principle, Truth,
in which there are not inharmonies
of sickness, pain or sin.

For matter is an error, there being no substance, which is Truth,
in a thing which changes and is
only that which belief makes it.

Christ was the Wisdom that
knew Truth dwelt not in opinion
that could be formed into any

Matter is mortal error.—page
169, edition of 1881.

The fundamental error of mortal
man is the belief that matter is intelligent.—page 122, edition of
1881.
Laws of matter are nothing more
or less than a belief of intelligence
and life in matter, which is the
procuring cause of all disease;
whereas God, Truth, is its positive
cure.—page 127, edition of 1881.
There is no life, truth, intelligence, or substance in matter.—
page 464, edition of 1898.

shape which the belief gave to it
and that the life which moved it
came not from it but was outside
of it.

It may be seen from the entire history of the Quimby-
Eddy debate that Mrs. Eddy and her followers have never
ceased to deny what they knew all along to be absolute fact.
Mrs. Eddy openly contradicted herself on numerous occasions
and has skillfully succeeded in somehow covering up the tremendous amount of deliberate trickery she utilized in trying
to discredit the Quimby Manuscripts. However, the fact stands
today, Miss Wilbur, Mr. Beasley and Christian Science notwithstanding, that to Phineas Parkhurst Quimby, *not* Mary Baker
Eddy, goes the dubious honor of being the "discoverer" of the
principles upon which Mrs. Eddy built her entire philosophical
superstructure. One only regrets that Christian Scientists
are not honest enough to give the credit to whom it rightfully
belongs, for history tells us there is no ground for denying it
since the Quimby Manuscripts have forever exploded one of
Mrs. Eddy's most fixed obsessions—the figment of Divine
Authorship.

CHAPTER IV

THE CHRISTIAN SCIENCE BIBLE

It is an inevitable conclusion, which follows from sound reasoning, that since Mrs. Eddy was the alleged heir apparent to Jesus Christ, her textbook, *Science and Health, With Key to the Scriptures*, should become the sacred oracle of her religion as the New Testament is of His. Since it is a fact questioned by comparatively few students of the movement's history that Mrs. Eddy at times claimed equality with Jesus, it follows that she should also claim for "her" teachings divine revelation or equality with the Bible. This she has irrevocably done. Wrote Mrs. Eddy in the *Christian Science Journal*, January, 1901:

> I should blush to write of *Science and Health, With Key to the Scriptures* as I have, were it of human origin and I apart from God its author, but as I was only a scribe echoing the harmonies of heaven in divine metaphysics, I cannot be super-modest of the Christian Science textbook.

Further than this brazen assertion of divine inspiration for her writings, Mrs. Eddy, in a personal letter to a friend in 1877, even then contended that her revelation of Christian Science was greater than the New Testament revelation—or as she said, "The idea given by God this time is higher, clearer and more permanent than before."[1]

It must be clear from this evidence that "Mother" Eddy was not to be bested by the Deity Himself, for since His initial

---

[1]*The Life of Mary Baker Eddy*, Georgine Milmine, p. 73. In later years Mrs. Eddy denied that she was equal to Jesus, yet quite often her own language and the glowing terms used to enshrine her memory by loyal Christian Scientists still leads the authors to believe that Mrs. Eddy is conceived of as being very close to deity and certainly second only to Christ.

revelation in Jesus Christ was not, in her own words, "permanent" enough, she undertook to improve upon it and thus insure its surviving the seas of time. Let it not be thought by any person reading this book that Mrs. Eddy did not personally aspire to equality with Jesus as some of her eager followers contend, because such a contention history brands as an utter falsehood. In the *Christian Science Journal,* April, 1889, Mrs. Eddy allowed the claim made in her behalf to the effect that she was the equal and chosen successor to Jesus Christ. Please notice that the *Christian Science Journal* was owned and published by her and nothing could creep into its copy without her personal approval. She therefore knew of the claim and allowed its circulation.* The facts speak for themselves. Knowing now as we do the attitude of Christian Scientists toward Mrs. Eddy and her writings, we shall examine her principal work, *Science and Health,* and see if what its "author" claimed for it is true—namely, that it equals if not supersedes the authority of the Bible and was dictated by God Almighty Himself.[2]

In any survey of *Science and Health,* the reader must keep three important thoughts paramount in his mind: (1) The terminology of *Science and Health* and some of its minor doctrinal vagaries are drawn from a little-known source in Mrs. Eddy's background—specifically her early experience with "the Shakers," a sect which flourished near her home in Tilton, New Hampshire (1836). (2) The current editions of *Science and Health* have undergone such thorough rewriting and professional polishing that grammatically and structurally they differ beyond comparison from the garbled, ungrammatical linguistic maze that was the first edition of 1875. (3) Mrs. Eddy has no respect whatsoever for the principles of logic,

---

*See also *Christ and Christmas,* a poem by Mrs. Eddy, edition of 1894, where she is by direct inference, and in unmistakable language accompanied by pictures, claimed to be Christ's equal co-worker.

[2]*The Religio-Medical Masquerade,* p. 57.

and contradictory premises and conclusions abound in her writings. The specific meanings of words also fade into oblivion where Mrs. Eddy is concerned, and terminology is often badly confused.

To alleviate the minds of many vociferous Christian Science apologists who disclaim Mrs. Eddy's ill-concealed debt to the Shakers, the authors list the following terms and doctrines she appropriated and subsequently enlarged upon:

Shakerism[3]	*Christian Science*
1. Shakers prayed to God and recognized the Deity as both masculine and feminine—"Our Father-Mother God."	1. Christian Science also adopted this as evidenced in Mrs. Eddy's version of the Lord's Prayer which begins: "Our Father-Mother God, all harmonious. . ." (*Science and Health*, p. 16).
2. The Prophetess of Shakerism, Ann Lee, was considered greater than Christ and was so revered by the Shakers.	2. Mrs. Eddy allowed herself to be represented as the equal and successor to Christ and was revered as such by many of her loyal followers continuing until today. She even at one point declared her mission superior to His[4] (*Religio-Medical Masquerade*, pp. 47 and 50-55; also *Christian Science Journal*, April, 1889).
3. The Shakers claimed Ann Lee, their leader, was the woman of the Apocalypse (Revelation 12).	3. Christian Science hails Mrs. Eddy as the same woman of the Apocalypse, and the "little book" as *Science and Health* (Revelation 10 and 12; and App. Cit. pp. 48-49).
4. Shakers sect gave to Ann Lee the endearing name "Mother" to denote her superiority and divine origin.	4. Christian Scientists "conferred" this title "Mother" upon Mary Baker Eddy, and she protected it by threatening excommunication to anyone daring to use it

---

[3]All quotations from Shaker beliefs are taken from Georgine Milmine, *The Life of Mary Baker Eddy*, pp. 494-495. All quotations from *Science and Health* are from the 1914 edition.
[4]Personal letter of Mary Baker Eddy, 1877.

5. The Shakers claim for Ann Lee the gift of miraculous healing powers.

in her church. (Manual 22, 1.). She also contradicted herself on this issue (see Mark Twain, *Christian Science*, pp. 335-336— "Mrs. Eddy in Error").

5. Christian Scientists and Mrs. Eddy herself claim that her powers were second only to Jesus Christ, if not equal to His (*Religio-Medical Masquerade*, pp. 103-106).

6. Shakers called their church—the Church of Christ.

6. Mrs. Eddy called hers the Church of Christ, Scientist. She merely added a word at the end (August 23, 1879).

7. The Shakers named their first church "The Mother Church."

7. Mrs. Eddy named her Boston edifice—The Mother Church (E. F. Dakin's *Mrs. Eddy*, p. 259).

8. Shaker cult was opposed in every way to audible prayer.

8. Mrs. Eddy taught that audible prayer is an inferior form and was against it generally (*Science and Health*, pp. 11 and 47).

9. The Shakers oppose marriage, considering it sinful, and encourage celibacy.

9. Mrs. Eddy gradually grew to be antagonistic toward marriage and held that it was "expedient" —"suffer to be so now" (*Miscellaneous Writings*, p. 286). She grew particularly bitter towards matrimony in her old age (85) and described it as synonymous with legalized lust (*Christian Science Sentinel*, June 16, 1906; *Christian Science Journal*, July, 1906).

It must be conceded, of course, that these similarities to Shakerism do not prove that Mrs. Eddy owed it a large debt, but merely one she and her followers were not willing to openly admit. But it is an interesting sidelight, nevertheless, to note this little-known fact of Christian Science history.

The true story of Mrs. Eddy's first literary effort, *Science*

and Health, With Key to the Scriptures, has been denied
by Christian Scientists universal since it was first revealed, and
subsequently allowed to slip into obscurity. Today one may
walk into any Christian Science reading room and purchase
a beautifully bound copy of *Science and Health* conveniently
divided into numbered verses and resembling in every way
possible a standard leather-bound Bible. In fact, the Bible
and *Science and Health* are consistently sold in matched
leather sets so that the faithful may have both copies of God's
revelations. The book itself is 700 pages long in its present
form, although at its first issue it was only 456 pages in length.
Through the years, especially 1886 to 1891, however, it has
undergone numerous changes and revisions which makes
today's copy a vastly different presentation than that of Mrs.
Eddy's own construction in 1875. Current editions of the book
contain fourteen chapters; in 1875 it had only eight and showed
little promise of success, but Mrs. Eddy was not to be denied,
and success eventually crowned her first efforts as an "author."
It would be a hopeless task to try and review all of *Science
and Health* in so short a space, and any review of it must be
both theological and philosophical by nature, since the entire
book is a mass of theological and philosophical propositions
in varying degrees. Chapter VI, therefore, is calculated to
survey these propositions and evaluate their worth—so we
shall defer comment upon such at the moment. We shall
instead examine the literary and historical background of
Science and Health which is nonetheless amazing even in
comparison to the Quimby Manuscript plagiarism. None can
honestly deny that although Mrs. Eddy wrote *Science and
Health,* she obtained her ideas from Quimby's writings; but
few persons outside the Christian Science hierarchy itself
know, that as Quimby fathered the ideas, so did James Henry
Wiggin, a retired Unitarian clergyman, render them at least
readable to the average person. Mr. Wiggin enjoyed the key

position of "literary adviser" to Mrs. Eddy from 1885 to 1891, nine years before his death in 1900. Through the efforts of Mr. Wiggin, Mrs. Eddy's work took on a professional tone completely foreign to her meager talents and abilities. In truth it was Mr. Wiggin who gave to *Science and Health* whatever logical philosophical propositions it contains, since Mrs. Eddy knew comparatively nothing of philosophy, theology, history, or the dead languages, and was therefore unable to write on such subjects intelligently. Mr. Wiggin kept all of these things to himself, unfortunately, and it was not until after his death, and then chiefly through the efforts of his "literary executor," Livingstone Wright, that his testimony and evidence in manuscript form was made public. Mr. Wiggin was well paid for his "ghost writing" chores and himself entertained a good-natured tolerance toward Mrs. Eddy, but he left more than enough evidence to show that he, not she, was the literary genius behind the early revisions of, and additions to, *Science and Health,* etc. To substantiate this beyond question, the authors reproduce below choice excerpts from an article by Livingstone Wright based upon and containing extensive quotations from Mr. Wiggin which most Christian Scientists find intensely distasteful. The reason for this is simple when one realizes that it is an unquestionably true and thoroughly documented exposé of Mrs. Eddy's false claims to divine revelation where *Science and Health* is concerned.

Should any person reading the following excerpts from Mr. Wright's article and Mr. Wiggin's statements entertain skepticism regarding the authenticity and truthfulness of the claims therein made, we should like to enter the following testimony as to the character of Mr. Wiggin himself into the record for all to see. The testimony is from no less an authority than Mary Baker Eddy, about whom Mr. Wiggin wrote, and concerning whom she made the following statement:

I hold the late Mr. Wiggin in loving, grateful memory for his high principled character and well-equipped scholarship (*First Church of Christ, Scientist and Miscellany,* p. 319).

It should be noted, therefore, that by her own words Mr. Wiggin had a "high principled character" and hence not given to outright falsehoods. Yet Mrs. Eddy denied that Mr. Wiggin did what he said he did, though she, Calvin Frye, her faithful secretary, and other selected contemporary Scientists knew Mr. Wiggin's statements, herein quoted, to be absolutely true.

However, further comment is fruitless beside the actual story itself, so from the Rev. J. H. Wiggin himself, here is the true, compelling story of the Christian Science Bible, factual evidence that has been pitifully neglected for over 40 years, and today is practically impossible to obtain.

The authors reproduce it here in the interest of the whole truth, free from Christian Science "interpretation."

How Rev. Wiggin Rewrote Mrs. Eddy's Book
or the
Peculiar Chapter in Christian Science
by Livingstone Wright

"This[5] hitherto unpublished Wiggin Chapter is the 'missing link' in Mrs. Eddy's propaganda; the chapter that explains what thousands of wondering critics have sought to know, namely: Why was it that about 1886 Mrs. Eddy's *Science and Health* and other[6] of her literary ventures took on a sudden veneer of pretended literary style and a polish entirely unknown to her previously published products? The Wiggin Chapter makes its own showing as to how it came about that at this period around 1886 Mrs. Eddy's propaganda flared forth to a success and importance entirely out of proportion to what might have been expected from the status of things preceding. It will suggest, perhaps, not only the means by which Mrs. Mary Morse Baker Glover Patterson Eddy suddenly learned to spell, but also, aside from his labors as a corrector and emitter of 'copy,' the work Wiggin achieved as Advisor-in-Chief and General Executive Counsel for Mrs. Eddy's labyrinthine enterprises.

"The Rev. James Henry Wiggin was born in 1836 at No. 19 Sheafe Street, in Boston's famous 'North End.' He died November 4, 1900,

[5]p. 11.
[6]p. 12

at his residence in Roxbury, Massachusetts. He was a direct descendant of Gov. Thomas Wiggin, who came to this country in 1631. In the 50's after a tutorship in a clergyman's family he entered Tufts College. With the resolve to become a minister, he entered the Meadville Theological School at the age of twenty-two and graduated in 1861. In 1862, while preaching at Montague, Massachusetts, he was ordained to the Unitarian ministry. Mr. Wiggin gave up regular pastoral duties in 1875, then confining himself to occasional lecturing, preaching and literary work.

"It[7] was in the latter part of December 1899, that the writer of this paper had a series of interviews with Rev. Mr. Wiggin.

" 'Late in August, 1885,' said Mr. Wiggin in beginning his statement, 'I received a call at my office in the old Boston Music Hall Building from a man who announced himself as "Calvin A. Frye." I was at the time quite actively engaged in the vocation of literary helper, advisor and critic. I had done work especially in the making of indices to books, making compilations and revisions and, in brief, was following the business of an author's aid.

"This Mr. Frye was very agreeable and suave in his manner, and gracefully explained that he was the secretary of a woman who had a book manuscript which she desired to have revised. He presented the matter in a very dignified manner, and I inferred from the tone of his remarks that the manuscript was probably in fair condition, at least as regarded the fundamental construction and arrangement—that is, the thought, the basic grammatical and literary element. That is to say, I supposed the work that I was being sought out to perform would consist of that which is the usual lot of the literary aid, namely, a general smoothing, careful attention to the punctuation, perhaps the tedious and painstaking work of preparing an index, and giving such literary advice and help as might be needed by an author of average education and literary ability. But, as I indicate presently, I little knew of the experience[8] in revision that I was destined to undergo. Mr. Frye left after I had agreed to meet the woman he represented, Mrs. Mary Baker Eddy, and have a talk with her.

Mrs. Eddy's Impressive Mien.

" 'A few days later she called on me. She was a person of quiet, stately mien, perfectly self-possessed and disposed to be somewhat ominous and impressive in manner. She had a huge package of manuscript which I learned was designed to serve as the material for a forthcoming edition of *Science and Health, With Key to the Scriptures.* We talked over the matter of recompense and those details, and she seemed satisfied with my terms; was very direct and business-like; and we entered into an arrangement whereby I was to undertake the revision of the manuscript, although she was careful to give me to

[7]p. 13.
[8]p. 14.

understand that she regarded herself as having already gotten the manuscript in approximately the proper shape for the printer. But there were, she confessed, "doubtless a few things here and there that would require the assistance of a fresh hand." I did not then give the package more than a mere passing glance.

"I was intending to go up to the mountains with my wife for a few days' vacation, and I put the package away in my satchel, thinking that when I got up in the hills I would set about the revision, which I supposed could be completed in a reasonably short time.

" 'Some days later I opened the package and began a scrutiny[9] of the manuscript. Well, I was staggered! Of all the dissertations a literary helper ever inspected, I do not believe one ever saw a treatise to surpass this. The misspelling, capitalization and punctuation were dreadful, but those things were not the things that feezed me. It was the thought and the general elemental arrangement of the work. There were passages that flatly and absolutely contradicted things that had preceded, and scattered all through were incorrect references to historical and philosophical matters. The things that troubled me were: How could I attempt to dress up this manuscript by dealing only with the spelling and punctuation? There would be left a mass of material that would reflect on me as a professional literary and were my name to be in any way associated with the enterprise, I saw, in a word, that the only way in which I could undertake the requested revision would be to begin absolutely at the first page and rewrite the whole thing. I tossed the package back into the satchel and did nothing more until I returned to Boston.

" 'I then had an interview with Mrs. Eddy and explained as kindly and gently as I could the situation as I found it. I told her I would have to rewrite the manuscript. I had rather expected something of a "scene" and was ready to tell her, as I had had occasion to tell one or two others in times past, that if I undertook the revision I must do so conscientiously, and that I could not be placed in a position where I might be censured[10] for a showing that was not my own.

" 'But instead of any hesitation or hint of annoyance, Mrs. Eddy in a calm, easy, thoroughly stately manner, agreed to my declaration about the matter of a re-write, acceded to my terms of recompense, and it began to slowly dawn upon me that perhaps this thing of a revision "from the ground up" as it were, was the very thing she had intended that I should do in the first place. In the course of our conversation I reiterated to her that she must understand, of course, that I was not a "Christian Scientist," did not hold views according to her own, and did not ever expect to become a "Christian Scientist." I wished this point to be thoroughly understood at the beginning, as I meant that literary revision and my own religious and ethical convictions should

[9]p. 15.
[10]p. 16.

have no affiliation one with the other. However, to all this, Mrs. Eddy
would respond in the blandest of manner: "Oh, we know you are not
a believer now, Mr. Wiggin, but we hope that you may come to unite
with us." And this continued to be her stereotyped comment whenever
the question of my own attitude toward Christian Science came up.

Wished Critics Could See It.

" 'Well, a clear understanding having been reached regarding the
way in which I was to do my revising, I set at work on that manuscript.
And I did work. I assure you that I often think now as I read the
ridicule of the critics concerning Mrs. Eddy's "literary style"[11] that I
wish they could have had a peep at that manuscript I was at work on
in the autumn of 1885. I think then they would have had something
to rave over.

" 'In speaking of my labors on Mrs. Eddy's books, I might make the
general observation that my most important mission, as I regard it, was
to, above all, accomplish two things: keep her from making herself
absolutely ridiculous, and, secondly, to keep her from flatly contradicting
herself. To gather an adequate conception of the problem that I undertook in revising that manuscript, one should have poured over the mass
of verbiage with me, day by day and page by page. The evidence of
lack of education and of ignorance concerning the writings and teachings
of the famous philosophers was so overwhelming that I could not trust
her references, but had to look up everything for myself to be sure
and to feel that I was doing work that was commendable to my own
standard and just to her while I remained her literary aid and counsel.

" 'It has been many times claimed for Mrs. Eddy, and she has
claimed it herself, that she knew something of the ancient languages
and literature. I can positively assure you that Mrs. Eddy knew nothing
whatever of the ancient languages. She could not translate a page of
Latin, Greek, Sanskrit, or give a synopsis of the teachings of the great
philosophers of the ancients were it to have saved her life. She was in
utter ignorance of those matters, and as for her knowledge of and
ability to write the English tongue, I think I have sufficiently[12] indicated
that at the beginning of my statement with regard to the manuscript.

" 'Thus it was that I tried to examine every sentence and to cut out
whenever she would permit it, for, understand, there were many occasions
when she insisted on using her particular words or expressions, even
though I had positively assured her that they had best be changed or
taken from the context; so, of course, in they went. I hunted up texts
and mottoes with which to head the various chapters and adorn or
illustrate the reading matter. All of this was a vagatelle, however,
compared to the maddening task of straightening out her weird English
and bolstering up her lack of learning, to use the mildest term. For

[11]p. 17.
[12]p. 18.

instance, there was a section to go in the chapter headed *"Healing and Teaching,"* and which will be found here on *page 360 of this copy of the sixteenth edition,* 1886, which is the edition that was made from this manuscript that I was revising. Barring the question of whatever sense or saneness this so-called "allegory" does have or does not have, that draft that I had seemed a hopeless commingling of efforts to gather legal terms and phrases and with no other result than a hodge-podge of law terms indiscriminately and improperly used. I worked and worked over this and finally got it in the shape you find it in the 16th edition.

" 'Another thing that I shall never forget was a chapter in which Mrs. Eddy had proceeded to arraign a group of physicians because her husband while under their[13] treatment had died. Mrs. Eddy accused these men of causing the death of Asa Gilbert Eddy by, to use her exact phrase, "arsonical poison mentally administered." She scored the doctors dreadfully in this essay of hers, and as there was nothing what-ever—an autopsy having been performed upon the deceased—to show any unprofessional, much less, criminal, conduct on the part of the attending physicians, who were of well-known and high-class reputation in their professions, I knew, of course, that the publication of any such charges as these would immediately bring her into serious trouble. I remonstrated with Mrs. Eddy about this chapter, but she seemed de-termined at first to have the chapter go in. I urged her to think well before she made any such preposterous charges as those in print. "You'll be arrested and convicted for criminal libel as surely as you print that accusation against those doctors," I declared. Mrs. Eddy replied that she "would think it over." I came later to learn that that was her way of preparing for assent to a point that she felt could not be safely carried. A few days later she asked me if I felt the same way about that chapter. "I certainly do," I answered. "Very well," she responded. Several days passed, when she once more asked me if I was still of the same opinion. I said "Yes." After the lapse of a few more days, she said to me: "Mr. Wiggin, I have decided to leave out that chapter."

Lord Spoke Through Wiggin.

" 'I felt relieved, as may be imagined, but was surprised[14] to hear her next statement. She said most impressively and with peculiar suavity of mien: *"Mr. Wiggin, I often feel as if the Lord spoke to me through you."*

" 'While I somewhat doubted the alleged fact of the Almighty employing me as a mouthpiece for the direction of Mrs. Eddy, never-theless there was a certain ominousness when she used to remind me, as

[13]p. 19.
[14]p. 20.

she later came to not infrequently, "that the Lord spoke to her through me."

" 'After many weary months on this manuscript, instead of the few weeks that I had supposed when this work was first suggested to me, the 16th edition, containing my revision of Mrs. Eddy's manuscript and a carefully prepared index, appeared in the early part of 1886.'

"Among the material that the late Rev. Wiggin turned over to the writer are two copies of *Science and Health, With Key to the Scriptures* of different editions and which are marked and crossed and annotated with the hand of the reviser in preparing for succeeding editions. The first of these is a copy of the 16th edition, 1886, and the second volume is that employed in preparing the revision (by Rev. Mr. Wiggin) for the *36th edition of* 1888. These volumes are now in the possession of the writer of this article. The markings point to an unmistakable conclusion regarding the intellectual and literary acquirement of Mrs. Eddy.

[15]" 'If you will examine the table of contents of these two volumes,' Mr. Wiggin said, 'you will find that they contain exactly the same number of pages, namely 590. You will notice that in the 16th edition the chapter captioned *"Animal Magnetism"* begins on page 211 and extends through to page 234, but in this other volume, the one I used in preparing the revision for the 36th edition of 1888, the chapter begins on page 211 but extends only to page 224, that is ten pages shorter. Now the reason for this is that there is an extra chapter in the latter volume, this chapter being entitled "Wayside Hints." This chapter has a history of its own.

" 'Mrs. Eddy had intended to get in something here about the alleged malpractice on the death of her husband, Asa Gilbert Eddy, but being persuaded by me as I have before indicated, to leave this subject entirely alone insofar as *Science and Health* was concerned, we had to have something to take the space she had intended to give that theme!

Wrote Sermon For Mrs. Eddy.

" 'Now, Mrs. Eddy was holding her meetings in a little hall. She used to preach each Sunday before a gathering of her followers and she had called upon me to draw up some outlines of sermons for her to use before this congregation. I drew up a sermon on the "Sacred City" that is described in Revelation, as the one that "hath foursquare." Mrs. Eddy took the sermon and I went down to the hall on the day she was to deliver[16] this sermon (my sermon) to her adherents. There was a large throng of women, and as Mrs. Eddy began to work in to the text, they began to be correspondingly enthused and enraptured. As I listened, and although Mrs. Eddy was doing pretty well, I must say, for a person who was striving to elaborate upon someone else's

---

[15]p. 21.
[16]p. 22.

plans and pulpit injunctions, she did get rather bungled up in trying to make the applications of the "four sides." Still the sermon as she delivered it seemed to impress her hearers as if it were a perfect, finished rhapsody, and all over the hall I could hear enthusiastic whispers of "Oh, isn't it grand!" "Oh, isn't she just divine!" "Oh, isn't she perfectly heavenly this morning!" "Oh, oh" and the like.

"'When Mrs. Eddy had concluded, and her ardent followers began to crowd around her for a word, a smile, a benediction or some vouch-safing of regard from the glorified one, I waited a few moments and as the enraptured "Oh's" and "Ah's" and the babble of feminine tongues flowed on, I made my way slowly toward the rostrum, and standing a little to one side, was awaiting some subsiding of the tumult of adenda-tion. When there did come a slight lull and while Mrs. Eddy was dis-tributing the blessed smiles to her flock, she suddenly caught sight of me, standing there with, I fear, some expression of amusement on my face. She suddenly clapped her hand over her mouth and shot the side whisper to me, "How did it go?"

"'"Oh, very well," I replied in an undertone, thoroughly[17] relishing the spectacle of these women having such joyous hysterics over my sermon, "very well."

"'When I got the opportunity, I said to Mrs. Eddy, "I have now the very thing for that vacant space! I will write out that sermon and we will put that into the book."

"'I wrote the sermon into a chapter for the book and called it "Wayside Hints." It appeared in editions of 1886 and followed on down through many editions. If I may cite a typical illustration, take the reference I made to a city: I say in this chapter that "A city conveys the idea of an assemblage of people for high purposes and is akin to another word, civilization, both coming from the Latin word civis (citizen) and civitas (city or states)." And further along on the same page you will notice that I say: "One can easily believe that our word polish is derived from polis, the Greek word for city." Now it must be understood that throughout these editions that I revised for Mrs. Eddy, as in the instances cited, from the chapter, "Wayside Hints," the mention of certain words being derived or probably derived from certain Latin or Greek words, is a matter due entirely to myself, for, as I have said, Mrs. Eddy had no familiarity whatever with the classics or classical tongues. The same is true with regard to most of the references to the philosophers and learned authorities. I am the one who worked them into the text. "Wayside Hints," how-ever, was so literally my own work[18] from beginning to end that I came to refer to it among the other chapters as "my chapter." I was considerably amused when a young Harvard student was telling me one day about his conversion to Christian Science through reading

[17]p. 23.
[18]p. 24.

Science and Health. He dilated at length upon one chapter namely, "Wayside Hints," whereupon I told him that that was my chapter.

" ' "Well," he said, "that was the very chapter that converted me!"

" 'As stated, this chapter ran on for a long, long time and through many editions of the book. One day Mrs. Eddy said to me:

" ' "Mr. Wiggin, whose chapter do you regard 'Wayside Hints'?"

" ' "Why, Mrs. Eddy, that is unquestionably my chapter! It consists of my own words from start to finish. It is most assuredly my chapter."

" 'Henceforth "Wayside Hints" ceased to be a part of the book known as *Science and Health, With Key to the Scriptures.*'

[19]["Who shall say Rev. J. Henry Wiggin was not a powerful aid to Mrs. Eddy?"]

Revised Her Other Writings.

"Mrs. Eddy was too shrewd a woman not to realize the mine that she had in Rev. J. Henry Wiggin, and we find that he soon came to occupy practically the position of general literary advisor and superintendent of literary detail over the entire range of Mrs. Eddy's publishing enterprises. He was shortly called upon to edit the official organ of the Christian Scientists and served for long periods, especially in 1887, 1888 and 1889, to carry on that work in connection with his labors at revising books for Mrs. Eddy. 'For,' said Mr. Wiggin, 'in addition to my revisions of *Science and Health, With Key to the Scriptures,* I revised and arranged many other publications for her, among them *Retrospection and Introspection, Miscellaneous Writings of Mrs. Eddy, Unity of Good, No and Yes,* and doctored her poems as well, *Christ and Christmas,* etc. Mrs. Eddy's "poems," by the way, were remarkable effusions. I know that a deal of sport has been made over[20] her "poems," attention having been drawn with some interest and amusement to the metre and the rhyming; . . . What the literary critics would have thought of the originals as they came into my hands from Mrs. Eddy— I surely don't know.'

A Word About the Quimby Manuscripts Controversy.

[21]"Since Mrs. Eddy had been reiterating in *Science and Health* that she 'discovered Christian Science in 1866' it can be realized what an annoyance to her was [22]the pamphlet of Dresser's,[23] and those quotations of her tremendous laudations of P. P. Quimby. These murmurings and accusations that she had borrowed her theories of 'Christian Science' from Quimby had been cropping forth for sometime, and had now

---

[19]p. 31.
[20]p. 35.
[21]p. 40.
[22]p. 41.
[23]Julius Dresser, "Dr." Quimby's successor, in the 1880's published a pamphlet proving that Mrs. Eddy owed her "discovery" of Christian Science to P. P. Quimby. The pamphlet is what Mr. Wiggin has reference to.

been wrought into a terrific broadside by Mr. Dresser. The haste and desperation with which Mrs. Eddy rushed to Mr. Wiggin, her general literary advisor, and declared 'This must be answered,' can be imagined. Here was something that struck at the very heart of Mrs. Eddy's propaganda.

"' "It must be answered," vociferated Mrs. Eddy to me,' said Mr. Wiggin. 'Accordingly I mentioned and cited to her point after point that Mr. Dresser had made. She could not deny them. Then I said to her: "Well, Mrs. Eddy, there is nothing to say." '

"Unable to get Mr. Wiggin to draft a reply, Mrs. Eddy determined, however, to make an 'answer' of her own, and in the *Christian Science Sentinel* of June, 1887, appeared the article. In this article, Mrs. Eddy, among other things, said of this P. P. Quimby, whom she had once glorified to the extremity of her vocabulary:

"'It was after the death of Mr. Quimby and when apparently at the door of death that I made this discovery in 1866. After that it took about ten years of hard work for me to reach the standard of my first edition of *Science and Health* published in 1875. As long ago as 1844 I was convinced that mortal mind produced[24] all disease and that various medical systems were in no proper sense scientific. In 1862, when I first visited Mr. Quimby, I was proclaiming to druggists and mesmerists that science must govern all healing.'

"The best she could do at refuting or explaining those newspaper articles was the following:

"'Did I write those articles purporting to be mine? I might have written them twenty or thirty years ago, for I was under the mesmeric treatment of Dr. Quimby from 1862 until his death in 1865. He was illiterate and I knew nothing then of the science of mind-healing, and I was as ignorant of mesmerism as Eve before she was taught by the serpent. Mind science was unknown to me, and my head was so turned by animal magnetism and will power, under this treatment, that I might have written something as hopelessly incorrect as the articles now published in the Dresser "pamphlet." '

"And yet, in the face of all this that she had once alleged for P. P. Quimby, in the face of such an 'answer' as the above, Mrs. Eddy has continued to reiterate until today through the editorials of *Science and Health* in her 'annual messages' to the 'Mother Church' and elsewhere that she 'discovered Christian Science in 1866.' And since the time that the Dresser pamphlet appeared, she has allowed herself to refer to Quimby, once so revered of her, as 'an ignorant mesmerist' and to term his manuscripts 'scribblings' and 'ignorant pennings.'

Mr. Wiggin Recalls Mrs. Eddy's Statement On Money.

[25]" 'Never but once, insofar as I can recollect, did this astute

---

[24]p. 42.
[25]p. 44-45.

woman "cross the line" as it were, and that was when she had one day made the usual expression of hope that I would join her church and I had made my customary refusal. She thereupon declared with unusual earnestness: "Mr. Wiggin, Christian Science is a good thing. I make ten thousand a year at it."

" 'Those were her very words. In all those years, beginning with the fall of 1885, that I was associated with her as literary advisor that was the only time when Mrs. Eddy got right down to the practical phase of her enterprise.'

"Such is a synopsis of the late Rev. J. Henry Wiggin's experience as general literary advisor to Mrs. Mary Baker Eddy.

"In speaking of Mr. Wiggin and Mrs. Eddy's book, W. G. Nixon of No. 15 Court Square, Boston, who was publisher of *Science and Health* for a long time, says:

" 'Mr. Wiggin made his last and a complete revision of *Science and Health* in 1891. He went over the whole business thoroughly that year. I took hold of *Science and Health* as Mrs. Eddy's publisher at the 44th edition in 1889, and met Wiggin in that year. I remained as Mrs. Eddy's publisher until the 74th edition in 1893. I can say that whatever style or literary polish is to be found in *Science and Health* is unquestionably due to Mr. Wiggin, for Mrs. Eddy certainly had no education requisite to the writing of a book, even in ordinary English. The cost of each copy of *Science and Health* to Mrs. Eddy was 47 cents.'

"If the reader of this article will take a pencil and do a little figuring he will gain some suggestion of the financial revenues that Christian Science has yielded its founder, if he accepts the statements of the Christian Science leaders that 'over 225,000 copies' of *Science and Health, With Key to the Scriptures* have been sold at from $3 to $5 a copy, the cost being *47 cents* a copy, and further bearing in mind that Mrs. Eddy has said she taught 'about five thousand students' in her 'Metaphysical College,' the advertised tuition in said 'college' being from $150 to $300 per student."

*   *   *

Having read Mr. Wiggin's testimony, that of a disinterested and honest man who for six years worked intimately with Mrs. Eddy, there can be little doubt that the intelligent person will see the picture clearly. Mrs. Eddy needed a literary advisor badly. Mr. Wiggin fitted the role admirably and, as a result, *Science and Health* showed for the first time in its history a semblance of literary congruity. But even Mr. Wiggin could not straighten out Mrs. Eddy's jumbled theology, and in a letter to a close friend, when speaking of Christian

Science, Mr. Wiggin gave what is probably the best thumb-nail sketch of the entire Christian Science religion ever written. Mr. Wiggin wrote:[26]

Christian Science, on its theological side, is an ignorant revival of one form of ancient gnosticism, that Jesus is to be distinguished from the Christ, and that His earthly appearance was phantasmal, not real and fleshly.

On its moral side, it involves what must follow from the doctrine that reality is a dream, and that if a thing is right in thought, why right it is, and that sin is non-existent, because God can *behold* no evil. Not that Christian Science believers generally see this, or practice evil, but the virus is within.

Religiously, Christian Science is a revolt from orthodoxy, but un-philosophically conducted, endeavoring to ride two horses.

Physically, it leads people to trust all to nature, the great healer, and so does some good. Great virtue in imagination! . . . Where there is disease which time will not reach, Christian Science is useless.

As for the High Priestess of it . . . she is—well, I could *tell* you, but not write, an awfully (I use the word advisedly) smart woman, acute, shrewd, but not well read, nor in any way learned. What she has, as documents clearly show, she got from P. P. Quimby of Port-land, Maine, whom she eulogized after death as the great leader and her special teacher.

. . . She tried to answer the charge of the adoption of Quimby's ideas and called me in to counsel her about it; but her only answer (in print!) was that if she said such things twenty years ago, she must have been under the influence of animal magnetism which is *her* devil. No church can long get on without a devil, you know. Much more I could say if you were here . . .

People beset with this delusion are thoroughly irrational. Take an instance. Dr. R . . . . . . of Roxbury is not a believer. His wife is. One evening I met her at a friendly house. Knowing her belief, I ventured only a mild and wary dissent, saying that I saw too much of it to feel satisfied, etc. In fact, the Doctor said the same and told me more in private. Yet, later, I learned that this slight discussion made her *ill*, nervous and had a bad effect.

One of Mrs. Eddy's followers went so far as to say that if she *saw* Mrs. Eddy commit a crime she should believe her own sight at fault, *not* Mrs. Eddy's conduct. An intelligent man told me in reference to lies he *knew* about, that the wrong was in *us*. "Was not Jesus accused of wrongdoing, yet guiltless?"

Only experience can teach these fanatics, i.e., the real believers,

[26]*The Life of Mary Baker Eddy and the History of Christian Science*, Georgine Mil-mine, pp. 337-339.

not the charlatans who go into it for money . . . As for the book, if
you have any edition since December, 1885, it had my supervision.
Though now she is getting out an entirely new edition with which I had
nothing to do and occasionally she had made changes whereof I did
not know. The chapter B. . . . . . told you of is rather fanciful, though,
to use Mrs. Eddy's language, in her last note, her "friends think it a
gem." It is the one called "Wayside Hints," and was added after the
work was not only in type, but cast, because she wished to take out
some twenty pages of diatribe on her dissenters . . . I do not think
it will greatly edify you, the chapter. As for clearness, many Christian
Science people thought her early editions much better, because they
sounded more *like* Mrs. Eddy. The truth is, she does not care to have
her paragraphs clear, and delights in so expressing herself that her
words may have various readings and meaning. Really, that is one of
the tricks of the trade. You know Sibyl's have always been thus oracular.
to "keep the word of promise to the ear, and break it to the hope."

There is nothing really to understand in *Science and Health* except
that *God is all,* and yet there is no God in matter! What they fail to
explain is, the origin of the *idea* of matter or sin. They say it comes
from *mortal mind,* and that mortal mind is not divinely created, in
fact, has no existence; in fact, nothing comes from nothing and that
matter and disease are like dreams, having no existence. Quimby had
definite ideas but Mrs. Eddy has not understood them.

When I first knew Christian Science, I wrote a defensive pamphlet
called *Christian Science and the Bible* (though I did not believe the
doctrine) . . . I found fair game in the assaults of orthodoxy upon
Mrs. Eddy, and support in the supernaturalism of the Bible; but I
did not pretend to give an exposition of Christian Science, and *I did
not know the old lady as well as I do now.*

No, Swedenborg, and all other such writers, are sealed books to
her. She cannot understand such utterances, and never could, but
dollars and cents she understood thoroughly.

Her influence is wonderful. Mrs. R——'s husband is anxious *not* to
have her undeceived, though her tenth cancer is forming, lest she
sink under the change of faith, and I can quite see that the loss of
such a faith, like loss of faith in a physician, might be injurious. . . .
In the summer of 1888, some thirty of her best people left Mrs. Eddy,
including her leading people, too, her association and church officers.
. . . They still believe nominally in Christian Science, yet several of
them . . . are studying medicine at the College of Physicians and
Surgeons, Boston; and she gave consent for at least *one* of them to
study at this allopathic school. These students I often see, and *they*
say the professors are coming over to *their* way of belief, which
means simply that they hear the trustworthiness of the laws of nature
proclaimed. As in her book, and in her class (which I went through)
she says, "Call a surgeon in surgical cases."

"What if I find a breech presentation in childbirth?" asked a pupil.
"You will *not*, if you are in Christian Science," replied Mrs. Eddy.
"But if I *do*?"
"Then send for the nearest regular practitioner."
You see, Mrs. Eddy is nobody's fool.

Summing up this chapter, the authors feel called upon to prove beyond question the fact that Mrs. Eddy often plagiarized her writings, and P. P. Quimby was not the only victim. Listed below in parallel columns are almost identical passages taken from *Murray's Reader*, a book in Mrs. Eddy's library, and a common publication of her era. The passages in question are quoted from the writings of a long-forgotten Scottish minister, Rev. Hugh Blair, which Mrs. Eddy no doubt thought appropriate as an "Annual message to the Mother Church." Such, therefore, it subsequently became, and is found on page 147 of her book, *Miscellaneous Writings*, as "her" annual message of 1895. Only a short introduction, and the elimination of a few words in the text serves to differentiate it from *Murray's Reader* as the interested reader will observe. Mrs. Eddy was also indebted at various times to Carlyle, Ruskin and Amiel, for numerous of "her" Philosophic Nuggets, and sound evidence is available to corroborate these facts.

Murray's Reader, p. 89.	*Miscellaneous Writings, p. 147.*
. . . the man of integrity . . . is one who makes it his constant rule to follow the road of duty, according as the word of God, and the voice of his conscience, point it out to him. He is not guided merely by affections, which may sometimes give the colour of virtue to a loose and unstable character.	The man of integrity is one who makes it his constant rule to follow the road of duty, according as Truth and the voice of his conscience point it out to him. He is not guided merely by affections which may some time give the color of virtue to a loose and unstable character.
2. The upright man is guided by a fixed principle of mind, which determines him to esteem nothing	The upright man is guided by a fixed Principle, which destines him to do nothing but what is honor-

but what is honourable; and to abhor whatever is base or unworthy, in moral conduct. Hence we find him ever the same; at all times, the trusty friend, the affectionate relation, the conscientious man of business, the pious worshipper, the public-spirited citizen.

3. He assumes no borrowed appearance. He seeks no mask to cover him, for he acts no studied part; but he is indeed what he appears to be, full of truth, candour, and humanity. In all his pursuits, he knows no path but the fair and direct one; and would much rather fail of success, than attain it by reproachful means.

4. He never shows us a smiling countenance, while he meditates evil against us in his heart. He never praises us amongst our friends; . . . We shall never find one part of his character at variance with another. . . . —*Blair.*

able, and to abhor whatever is base or unworthy; hence we find him ever the same—at all times the trusty friend, the affectionate relative, the conscientious man of business, the pious worker, the public-spirited citizen.

He assumes no borrowed appearance. He seeks no mask to cover him, for he acts no studied part; but he is indeed what he appears to be,—full of truth, candor and humanity. In all his pursuits, he knows no path but the fair, open, and direct one, and would much rather fail of success than attain it by reproachable means. He never shows us a smiling countenance while he meditates evil against us in his heart. We shall never find one part of his character at variance with another. Lovingly yours,

Mary Baker Eddy

Sept. 30, 1895

The authors feel sure that the foregoing evidence clearly shows that Mrs. Eddy was not beyond stooping to plagiarism whether Quimby or the Rev. Mr. Blair, and this example of her handiwork leaves even her most devout followers little defense for her scholastic dishonesty as evidenced by their peculiar silence on this issue.

Chapter V

The Theology of Christian Science

The inclusion of this chapter which contains basic quotations from Mrs. Eddy's writings, hence a thorough presentation of Christian Science theology, is designed to clarify the views of Mrs. Eddy and Christian Science and to present them devoid of any comment whatsoever on the part of the authors. In brief, it is our desire and purpose to outline, using standard doctrinal headings when possible, the principal dogmas of Christian Science, that a clear concept of what this philosophy teaches may be understood by all. The following is therefore the official Christian Science interpretation of theology which every loyal Christian Scientist must adhere to or be liable to loss of church membership:

I. Inspiration of the Bible.

1. . . . "the Scriptures cannot properly be interpreted in a literal way . . . the literal rendering of the Scriptures makes them nothing valuable, but often is the foundation of unbelief and hopelessness" *(Miscellaneous Writings,* p. 169).*

2. "The material record of the Bible . . . is no more important to our well being than the history of Europe and America" *(Miscellaneous Writings,* p. 170).

3. Referring to Genesis 2:7: "Is this addition to His creation real or unreal? Is it the truth? Or is it a lie, concerning man and God? It must be the latter . . ." *(Science and Health,*[1] p. 517).

---

*All quotations from *Miscellaneous Writings* are from the edition of 1897.
[1] All quotations from *Science and Health* are from the edition of 1895 unless specifically designated otherwise.

4. Referring to Genesis 3:22: "This could not be the utterance of truth or science . . . the translators of this record of Scientific creation entertained a false sense of Being. They believed in the existence of matter, its propagation and power. From that standpoint of error, they could not apprehend the nature and operation of spirit" (*Science and Health*, p. 537).

5. ". . . the manifest mistakes in the ancient versions; the thirty thousand different readings in the Old Testament, and the three hundred thousand in the New,—these facts show how a mortal and material sense stole into the divine record, darkening, to some extent, the inspired pages with its own hue" (*Science and Health*, p. 33).

II. The Doctrine of the Trinity
and the Deity of Christ.

1. "The theory of three persons in one God (that is, a personal Trinity or Tri-unity) suggests heathen gods, rather than the one ever-present I AM" (*Science and Health,* p. 152).

2. "The Christian who believes in the First Commandment is a monotheist. Thus he virtually unites with the Jews' belief in one God and recognizes that Jesus Christ *is not God* as Jesus Himself declared, but is the Son of God" (*Science and Health,* Edition of 1914, p. 361).

3. "God is Good, . . . God is the only Life, . . . God is All-in-all . . . God is individual, incorporeal, the universal Cause . . . God is all-inclusive . . . He fills all space . . . Life, Truth, and Love constitute the triune God, or triply divine Principle . . . God the Father; Christ the type of Sonship; Divine Science, or the Holy Comforter" (*Science and Health*, pp. 226-227).

4. "The spiritual Christ was infallible; Jesus, as material manhood, *was not* Christ" (*Miscellaneous Writings*, p. 84).

5. "If there had never existed such a person as the Galilean prophet it would make no difference to me. I should still know that God's spiritual ideal is the only real man in his image and likeness" (*The First Church of Christ, Scientist and Miscellany,* pp. 318-319).

III. The Doctrine of God and the Holy Spirit.

1. "In that name of Jehovah the true idea of God seems almost lost. He becomes 'a man of war,' a tribal god to be worshipped,—rather than Love, the divine Principle to be lived and loved" (*Science and Health,* p. 517).
2. "In divine Science the terms God and good as Spirit are synonymous" (*Miscellaneous Writings,* p. 27).
3. "The Principle of Divine Metaphysics is God; . . . It reverses all perverted and physical hypotheses concerning Deity" (*Science and Health,* p. 5).
4. "GOD: Principle, Life, Truth, Love, Soul, Spirit, Mind" (*Science and Health,* p. 9).
5. "God is the Principle of all that represents Him, and of all that really exists" (*Science and Health,* p. 169).
6. "God is all . . . the soul, or mind, of the spiritual man *is* God, the divine Principle of all being" (*Science and Health,* Edition of 1914, p. 302).
7. "God is the Principle of Man; and the Principle of man remaining perfect" (*Science and Health,* p. 466).
8. "God. . . the all-knowing, all-seeing, all-acting, all-wise, all-loving, and eternal; Principle; Mind; . . . Substance; Intelligence" (*Science and Health,* p. 578).
9. "Mother. God; divine and eternal Principle, Life, Truth, and Love" (*Science and Health,* p. 583).
10. "Holy Ghost. Divine Science; the developments of eternal Life, Truth, and Love" (*Science and Health,* p. 579).
11. "Holy Ghost,—that influx of Divine Science . . . is now repeating its ancient history" (*Science and Health,* p. 348).

12. "In the words of St. John: 'He shall give you another Comforter, that he may abide with you forever.' This Comforter I understand to be divine Science" (*Science and Health*, Edition of 1914, p. 55).

IV. THE VIRGIN BIRTH OF CHRIST.

1. "A portion of God could not enter corporeal mortal man; neither could His fulness be reflected by Him, or God would be manifestly finite, lose the deific character, and become less than God" (*Science and Health*, p. 231).

2. "The Virgin-mother conceived this idea of God, and gave to her ideal the name of Jesus—that is, Joshua, or Saviour" (*Science and Health*, p. 334).

3. "Jesus, the Galilean prophet, was born of the virgin Mary's spiritual thoughts of life and its manifestation" (*The First Church of Christ, Scientist and Miscellany*, p. 261).

V. THE MEANING OF MIRACLES AND HEALING.

1. "Jesus cast out devils, mediating between what is and is not until a perfect consciousness is obtained. He healed disease as He healed sin; but He treated them both, not as in or of matter, but as mortal beliefs to be exterminated" (*No and Yes*, Edition of 1893, pp. 40-41).

2. "The sick are not healed merely by declaring there is no sickness, but by knowing that there is none" (*Science and Health*, Edition of 1914, p. 447).

3. "A mere request that God will heal the sick has no power to gain more of the divine presence than is always at hand" (*Science and Health*, p. 317).

4. "This common custom, of praying for the recovery of the sick, finds help in blind belief; whereas help should come from the enlightened understanding. . . . If the sick recover because they pray, or are prayed for audibly, only

petitioners (*per se* or by proxy) should get well" (*Science and Health,* p. 318).

5. "The so-called miracles contained in Holy Writ are neither supernatural or preternatural; . . . Jesus regarded good as the normal state of mind and evil as the abnormal. . . . The so-called pains and pleasures of matter were alike unreal to Jesus; for He regarded matter as only a vagary of mortal belief, and subdued it with this understanding" (*Miscellaneous Writings,* pp. 200-201).

6. "The blood, heart, lungs, brain, etc., have nothing to do with Life" (*Science and Health,* p. 45).

VI. THE ATONEMENT OF JESUS CHRIST.

1. "The material blood of Jesus was no more efficacious to cleanse from sin, when it was shed upon 'the accursed tree,' than when it was flowing in His veins, as He went daily about His Father's business" (*Science and Health,* p. 330).

2. "Does erudite theology regard the crucifixion of Jesus as chiefly providing a ready pardon for all sinners who ask for it, and are willing to be forgiven? . . . Then we must differ. . . The efficacy of the crucifixion lies in the practical affection and goodness it demonstrated for mankind" (*Science and Health,* p. 329).

3. "The real atonement—so infinitely beyond the heathen conception that God requires human blood to propitiate His justice and bring His mercy—needs to be understood. . . . He (Jesus) suffered, to show mortals the awful price paid by sin and how to avoid paying it. He atoned for the terrible unreality of a supposed existence apart from God. He suffered because of the shocking human idolatry that presupposes Life, Substance, Soul, and Intelligence in matter. . ." (*No and Yes,* pp. 44-45)—Edition of 1893.

VII. The Death and Resurrection of Christ.

1. "Resurrection. Spiritualization of thought; a new and
   higher idea of immortality, or spiritual existence; material
   belief, yielding to spiritual understanding" (*Science and
   Health,* p. 584).
2. "Our Master fully and finally demonstrated Divine Science,
   in its victory over death and the grave. . . . Glory be to
   God and peace to the struggling hearts! Christ hath rolled
   away the stone from the door of human hope and faith,
   and elevated them to possible at-one-ment with the spiritual idea and its divine Principle, through the revelation
   and demonstration of Life in Divine Science!" (*Science
   and Health,* p. 350).
3. "Jesus' students, not sufficiently advanced to fully understand their Master's triumph, did not perform many wonderful works until they saw Him after His crucifixion, and
   learned that *He had not died*" (*Science and Health,* p.
   350-351).
4. "To accommodate Himself to immature ideas of spiritual
   power. . . . Jesus called the body, which by this power
   He raised from the grave, 'flesh and bones' " (*Science and
   Health,* p. 209).
5. "The belief that material bodies return to dust, hereafter
   to rise up as spiritual bodies with material sensations and
   desires, is incorrect" (*Science and Health,* Edition of 1914,
   p. 73).
6. "His disciples believed Jesus dead while He was hidden
   in the sepulchre; whereas He was alive, demonstrating,
   within the narrow tomb, the power of Spirit to destroy
   human, material sense" (*Science and Health,* p. 349).

VIII. The Ascension and Second Coming of Christ.

1. "Through all the disciples beheld, they became more

may lead us into temptation" (*Science and Health,* pp. 312-313).

XIV. THE CREATION OF MATTER AND ITS REALITY.

1. "If God is Spirit, and God is All, surely there can be no matter. . . . According to Christian Science the first idolatrous claim of sin is, that matter exists; the second that matter is Substance; the third, that matter has intelligence, and the fourth, that matter, being so endowed, produces life and death. . . . By matter is commonly meant mind— not the highest Mind, but a false form of mind. . . . God is All, and God is Spirit; therefore there is nothing but Spirit; and consequently there is no matter . . . Matter is the opposite of Spirit, . . . hence, that matter is erroneous, transitory, unreal" (*Unity of Good,* pp. 39, 40, 43, 45).— Edition of 1898.

2. "Matter has no life to lose, . . . Therefore it is neither substantial, living, nor intelligent" (*Science and Health,* p. 171).

3. "Error is a supposition that pleasure and pain—that intelligence, substance, life—are existent in matter" (*Science and Health,* p. 468).

4. "Matter is but the subjective state of mortal mind. Matter has no more substance and reality in our day-dreams than it has in our night-dreams" (*First Church of Christ, Scientist and Miscellany,* p. 109).

5. "There is . . . no intelligent sin, evil mind or matter: and this is the only true philosophy and realism" (*No and Yes,* p. 47).

6. "The real Christ was unconscious of matter, of sin, disease, and death, and was conscious only of God, of Good, of eternal Life and harmony" (*No and Yes,* p. 45).

7. "There is no Life, Truth, intelligence or substance in matter but all is infinite Mind and its infinite manifestation for

God is All in all" (*Science and Health*, Edition of 1914, p. 468).

XV. Man, the Soul, His True Nature and Character.

1. "Man is not matter,—made up of brains, blood, bones, and other material elements. . . Man is spiritual and perfect; and because of this, he must be so understood in Christian Science. . . Man is incapable of sin, sickness, and death, inasmuch as he derives his essence from God. . ." (*Science and Health*, p. 471).

2. "If Soul sins, it must be mortal. . . Soul is the divine Principle of man, and never sins. Hence the immortality of Soul. In Science we learn it is material sense, not Soul, which sins; and it will be found that it is the sense of sin which is lost, and not a sinful soul" (*Science and Health*, p. 477).

3. "Man originated not from dust, materially, but from Spirit, spiritually" (*Miscellaneous Writings*, p. 57).

4. "God creates man perfect and eternal in his own image. Hence man is the image, idea, or likeness of perfection— an idea which cannot fall from its inherent unity with divine Love, from its spotless purity and original perfection (*The First Church of Christ, Scientist and Miscellany*, p. 262).

5. ". . . Man is the ultimate of perfection, and by no means the medium of imperfection. . . . If God is upright and eternal, man as His likeness is erect in goodness and perpetual in Life, Truth, and Love. . . . The spiritual man is that perfect and unfallen likeness, co-existent and co-eternal with God" (*Miscellaneous Writings*, p. 79).

6. "Man is God's image and likeness; whatever is possible to God, is possible to man as God's reflection" (*Miscellaneous Writings*, p. 183).

7. "In Science there is no fallen state of being; for therein is

no inverted image of God, no escape from the focal radia-
tion of the Infinite" (*No and Yes,* p. 26).

XVI. THE EXISTENCE OF SIN, SICKNESS AND DEATH.

1. "To regard sin, disease, and death with less deference, and
   only as the woeful unrealities of being, is the only way to
   destroy them. . ." (*Miscellaneous Writings,* p. 60).

2. ". . . God is all and He is Good, and Good is Spirit; hence
   there is no intelligent sin, evil *mind,* or matter: and this
   is the only true philosophy and realism" (*No and Yes,*
   p. 47).

3. "Being destroyed, sin needs no other form of forgiveness.
   . . . Since God is All, there is no room for His opposite.
   . . . therefore evil, being the opposite of goodness, is unreal, . . . for the sinner is making a reality of sin—making
   that real which is unreal, . . . Only those who repent of
   sin, and forsake all evil, can fully understand the unreality
   of evil. . . . To get rid of sin, through Science, is to divest
   sin of any supposed mind or reality, and never to admit
   that sin can have intelligence or power, pain or pleasure.
   You conquer error by denying its verity" (*Science and
   Health,* p. 234).

4. "Death. An illusion, for there is no death; the unreal and
   untrue; the opposite of Good, God, or Life. . . Any material
   evidence of death is false, for it contradicts the spiritual
   facts of Being" (*Science and Health,* p. 575).

5. ". . . to understand that sickness is a delusion, and that
   Truth can destroy it, is best of all, for it is the universal
   and perfect remedy" (*Science and Health,* p. 392).

6. "Sin, disease and death have no foundations in Truth"
   (*Science and Health,* p. 413).

7. "To put down the claim of sin you must detect it, remove
   the mask, point out the illusion, and thus get the victory

over sin, and prove its unreality" (*Science and Health*, p. 444).

8. ". . . Matter and evil (including all inharmony, sin, disease, death) are unreal" (*Miscellaneous Writings*, p. 27).

9. "Human mind produces what is termed organic disease as certainly as it produces hysteria. . ." (*Science and Health*, p. 69).

10. "The beliefs of the human mind rob and enslave it, and then impute this result to another elusive personification, named Satan . . . The belief of sin, which has grown terrible in strength and influence, is an unconscious error in the beginning—an embryotic thought without motive; but afterwards it governs the so-called man" (*Science and Health*, p. 81).

XVII. Animal Magnetism.

1. "As used in Christian Science, *animal magnetism* is the specific term for error, or mortal mind. It is a belief that mind is material, and both evil and good . . ." (*Science and Health*, p. 283).

2. "Mortal mind, acting from the basis of sensuous belief in matter, is animal magnetism . . ." (*Science and Health*, p. 71).

3. "Animal magnetism is the voluntary or involuntary action of error in all its forms, and is the human antipodes of Divine Science" (*Science and Health*, p. 480).

4. "The only incentive of a mistaken sense is malicious animal magnetism,—the name of all evil—and this must be understood" (*First Church of Christ, Scientist and Miscellany*, p. 357).

5. ". . . Animal magnetism is the highest form of mental evil, wherewith to complete the sum total of sin" (*First Church of Christ, Scientist and Miscellany*, p. 212).

* * *

Concluding this outline of Christian Science theology, the authors include below a brief chart vital, we believe, to an understanding of Mrs. Eddy's works and one which, in our opinion, is equally essential to a thorough refutation of Christian Science. This chart contains a list of common Biblical terms, the meanings of which Mrs. Eddy has changed to accommodate her innumerable literary mazes and confused terminology. Any standard Bible dictionary or secular work, for that matter, will reveal quickly to the interested reader that Mrs. Eddy has done immeasurable violence to the meanings of words and especially those found in Biblical contexts. We defer the final evaluation as always to the reader who can see for himself the indescribable confusion which Christian Science terminology predicates. The following definitions are taken from the Glossary of Mrs. Eddy's textbook, *Science and Health, With Key to the Scriptures*, Edition of 1895, pages 570-590 unless designated otherwise:

1. "*Adam.* Error; a falsity; the belief in 'original sin,' sickness and death; evil; the opposite of Good, . . . a curse; a belief in intelligent matter, . . . the first god of mythology. . . ."
2. "*Angels.* God's thoughts passing to man; spiritual intuitions, pure and perfect. . . ."
3. "*Ark.* Safety; . . . The Ark also shows that temptation, if overcome, is followed by exaltation."
4. "*Baptism.* . . . . submergence in Truth."
5. "*Burial.* Corporeality and physical sense put out of sight and hearing; annihilation; submergence in Spirit. . . ."
6. "*Children.* Life, Truth, and Love's spiritual thoughts and representatives; . . . sensual and mortal beliefs; counterfeits of creation, whose better originals are God's thoughts, not in embryo, but in maturity. . . ."
7. "*Christ.* The divine manifestation of God, which comes in the flesh, to destroy incarnate error."
8. "*Creator.* Spirit; Mind; Intelligence; the animating Prin-

ciple of all that is real and good; . . . God, who made all that was made, and could not create an atom or an element the opposite of Himself."

9. "*Dan* (Jacob's son). Animal magnetism; so-called mortal mind controlling mortal mind; error, working out the designs of error. . . ."

10. "*Day*. The irradiance of Life; light, the spiritual idea of Truth and Love."

11. "*Death*. An illusion, for there is no death; the unreal and untrue; the opposite of Good, God, or Life. Matter has no life, and hence it has no real existence. Mind is immortal."

12. "*Devil*. Evil; a lie; error; neither corporeality nor mind; the opposite of Truth; a belief in sin, sickness, and death. . . ."

13. "*Ears*. Not organs of the so-called corporeal senses, but spiritual understanding."

14. "*Earth*. . . To material sense, earth is matter; to spiritual sense, it is a compound idea."

15. "*Eve*. A beginning; mortality; . . . a finite belief concerning life, substance, and intelligence in matter; error; the belief that the human race originated materially instead of spiritually. . . ."

16. "*Evening*. Mistiness of mortal thought; weariness of mortal mind; obscured views; peace and rest."

17. "*Father*. Eternal Life; the one Mind; the divine Principle, commonly called God."

18. "*Flesh*. An error of physical belief; . . . an illusion; a belief that matter has sensation."

19. "*God*. The great I AM; the all-knowing, all-seeing, all-acting, all-wise, all-loving, and eternal; Principle; Mind; Soul; Spirit; Life; Truth; Love; Substance; Intelligence."

20. "*Good*. God; Spirit; omnipotence; omniscience; omnipresence; omni-action."

21. "*Heaven*. Harmony; the reign of Spirit; government by Principle; . . . the atmosphere of Soul."

22. "*Hell*. Mortal belief; error; lust; remorse; hatred; sin; sickness; death; . . . self-imposed agony; . . . that which 'maketh and worketh a lie.'"

23. "*Holy Ghost*. Divine Science; the developments of eternal Life, Truth and Love."

24. "*Jesus*. The highest human corporeal concept of the divine idea. . . ."

25. "*Lamb of God*. The spiritual idea of Love; self-immolation; innocence and purity; sacrifice."

26. "*Lord God*. Jehovah. This double term is not used in the first chapter of Genesis, the record of *spiritual* creation. It is introduced in the second and following chapters, when the spiritual sense of God and infinity are *disappearing* from the recorder's thought,—when the true Scientific statements of the Scriptures become clouded, through a physical sense of God as finite and corporeal. From this follow idolatry and mythology,—belief in many gods, or material intelligences, as the opposite of the one Spirit, or Intelligence, named Elohim, or God."[2]

27. "*Man*. The infinite idea of infinite Spirit; . . . the full representation of Mind."

28. "*Matter*. Mythology; mortality; . . . illusion; . . . the opposite of Truth; . . . the opposite of God. . . ."

29. "*Mind*. The only I, or Us; the only Spirit, Soul, Principle, Substance, Life, Truth, Love; the one God; . . .God, of whom man is the full and perfect expression. . . ."

30. "*Mother*. God; divine and eternal Principle, Life, Truth, and Love."

31. "*New Jerusalem*. Divine Science; the spiritual facts of the

---

[2]Mrs. Eddy's false conception that Elohim, the Hebrew plural for God, is the true God and that Jehovah, the absolute name of Deity, is a false divinity which "clouded" the Scriptures (Genesis 2 following) stems from the fact that she was totally ignorant of the Hebrew language which innumerable times in the Old Testament *combines* both terms, Jehovah and Elohim, into the compound Lord God. The play on words, therefore, by Mrs. Eddy is merely a weak excuse for her lack of Biblical education.

universe, . . . the Kingdom of Heaven, or reign of harmony."

32. "*Night*. Darkness; doubt; fear" (*Science and Health*, Edition of 1914, p. 592).

33. "*Resurrection*. Spiritualization of thought; a new and higher idea of Immortality, or spiritual existence; material belief, yielding to spiritual understanding."

34. "*Reuben* (Jacob's son). Corporeality; sensuality; delusion; mortality; error."

35. "*River*. Channel of thought."

36. "*Salvation*. Life, Truth, and Love, understood and demonstrated as supreme over all. . . ."

37. "*Serpent*. . . . a lie; the opposite of Truth, named error; . . . the first claim that sin, sickness, and death are the realities of life."

38. "*Shem* (Noah's son). . . . kindly affection; Love rebuking error; reproof of sensualism."

39. "*Spirit*. Divine Substance; Mind; Principle; all that is Good; God. . . ."

40. "*Spirits*. Mortal beliefs; corporeality; mortal men and women; supposed intelligences, . . . the opposites of God; errors; hallucinations."

41. "*Sun*. The symbol of Soul governing man,—of Truth, Life, and Love."

42. "*Sword*. The idea of Truth; justice; revenge; anger."

43. "*Wilderness*. Loneliness; doubt; darkness. . . ."

44. "*Will*. The motive-power of error; belief; animal power; the might and wisdom of God."

45. "*Wine*. Inspiration; understanding; error; fornication; temptation; passion."

46. "*Zion*. Spiritual foundation and superstructure; inspiraration; spiritual strength; emptiness; unfaithfulness; desolation."

❊ ❊ ❊

After reading this almost unbelievable travesty by Mrs. Eddy upon the meaning of simple Biblical terminology, it is inconceivable that the balanced mind will not revolt against so deplorable a perversion of obvious facts. Christian Science deliberately changes the clear meanings of innumerable Biblical terms to fit into the Eddy theology, which survives chiefly because its adherents seem incapable of logical thought where Biblical issues are concerned. The endless and palpably absurd language, grammar, and construction of *Science and Health* is represented by Christian Scientists as "marvelous truth" and is declared to be incomprehensible only to those whose minds are not enlightened by the Eddy revelation. But this, unfortunately for Christian Science, is not the whole case. The authors have time and again sat in Christian Science congregations and seen apparently intelligent persons smiling contentedly under the ministry of the various "readers," who recite in melodious tones portions of Mrs. Eddy's work entirely foreign to the understanding of anyone present—including those reading it! It is obvious from the book itself that Mrs. Eddy had difficulty in understanding her own thoughts which are a veritable hodgepodge of contradictory premises and false conclusions. It is a sick and darkened soul indeed that can rob God the Father of His Personality, God the Son of His deity, God the Holy Spirit of His ministry, and the Word of God itself of its authority and power. These things Mrs. Eddy has attempted to do and all Christian Scientists contribute to her guilt by accepting her false religion and the monstrous fabrications which make up the greater part of Christian Science theology. Thoughtful persons can only earnestly hope and pray that this darkness may be dispelled in the Lord's own good time and through the grace of Him who is the true light of the world (John 8:12).

Chapter VI

A Refutation of Christian Science Theology

The purpose of this chapter is the presentation of a point-by-point Biblical refutation of Christian Science theology designed to show the interested reader the main reasons why Christian Science is *not* a Christian religion. Before beginning this apologetic survey, however, the authors believe it necessary that the philosophic structure of the Eddy religion be thoroughly understood. In keeping with this belief we have undertaken a brief exposition of Mrs. Eddy's theory of knowledge and one we feel sure all philosophers and logicians, amateur or professional, will appreciate.

The philosophy of Christian Science is basically a syllogistic[1] one embodying all the logical mazes that the confused and untrained mind of Mrs. Eddy wandered through. Theoretically Mrs. Eddy was an Absolute Idealist who denied outright the existence of matter from the tiniest insect to the most gigantic star in the celestial galaxies. But practically speaking Mrs. Eddy was a calculating materialist, an individual who thoroughly enjoyed all the material comforts derived from denying their existence. Hundreds of thousands of faithful Christian Scientists supplied their "leader" with all that money could buy, and every material benefit available, yet Mrs. Eddy continually affirmed the non-existence of these material blessings by teaching in effect that they really did not exist to be enjoyed—they were "illusions of mortal mind," she said. In Mrs. Eddy's philosophy all that exists is "Mind" (God) and "It" is "Good"; matter has no "real" existence at all. It should be mentioned here that Mrs. Eddy never defined matter

---

[1]Syllogism (in logic)—"a form of argument or reasoning, consisting of two statements and a conclusion drawn from them" (dictionary).

to the satisfaction of any qualified logician, that is, so it must be assumed that she meant those elements which were recognizable to the five senses of man, etc.

The core of Christian Science philosophy is found in Mrs. Eddy's own textbook, *Science and Health*, Edition 1895, page 7, where in simple language, for a refreshing change, Mrs. Eddy states her basic tenets:

The fundamental propositions of Christian Science are summarized in the four following, to me, *self-evident* propositions. Even if read backward, these propositions will be found to agree in statement and proof.

1. God is All.
2. God is Good. God is Mind.
3. God, Spirit, being all, nothing is matter.
4. Life, God, omnipotent Good, deny death, evil, sin, disease.— Disease, sin, evil, death, deny Good, omnipotent God, Life.

Which of the denials in Proposition Four is true? Both are not, cannot be true. According to the Scripture, I find that God is true, "and every (mortal) man a liar."

The metaphysics of Christian Science, like the rules of mathematics, prove the rule by inversion. For example: There is no pain in Truth, and no truth in pain; no matter in Mind, and no mind in matter; no nerves in Intelligence, and no intelligence in nerves; no matter in Life, and no life in matter; no matter in Good, and no good in matter.

From this interesting statement of Mrs. Eddy's the observant reader will doubtless notice three important things:

1. Mrs. Eddy is fond of using "reversible propositions," especially those that interchange her names for Deity.

2. The rule of inversion is a common criterion for determining Christian Science "truth"—merely invert a proposition and prove its metaphysical validity, Mrs. Eddy teaches.

3. False premises and conclusions, as well as downright illogical propositions, abound in Mrs. Eddy's system.

The reversible propositions, so trumpeted by Mrs. Eddy in her "fundamentals," are by nature most damaging to her whole philosophic structures since they are demonstrably unreliable when applied to everyday practical experiences. For example, Mrs. Eddy says:

"God is all; (reversed) "All is God.""

or

"Good is Mind;" (reversed) "Mind is Good," etc. But let us further apply her "reversed proposition" standard and test its reliability:

1. Sleep is relaxation—(reversed) relaxation is sleep. (This is not always so; simply reclining or indulging in mild forms of exercise are often methods and forms of relaxation.)

2. Electricity is energy—(reversed) energy is electricity. (Basic laws of physics flatly contradict such a conclusion since energy takes many forms and cannot be confined to electricity alone.)

3. Death is immobility—(reversed) immobility is death. (This is of course untrue since an individual can be either asleep or paralyzed by disease, hence immobile and not at all dead.)

With these simple examples of how undependable the practice of reversing propositions is, we shall now examine Mrs. Eddy's rule of inversion strongly akin to her reversible proposition theory.

According to Mrs. Eddy "there is no pain in Truth, and no truth in pain; no matter in Mind, and no mind in matter, etc." (page 7) and this is "proved" metaphysically by the rule of inversion. However Mrs. Eddy's vaunted metaphysical allegiance to this alleged rule crumbles weakly under the relentless hammering of sound logical principles. Let us see if the rule of inversion is always valid by applying it to similar constructions.

All rabbits are quadrupeds—(inverted) all quadrupeds are rabbits. Now of course any intelligent person can easily see that this inversion leads to a false conclusion since dogs, cats, horses and elephants are all quadrupeds and it is obvious they have no relation to the rabbit family. No rational person could therefore long entertain such logical absurdity, but it is exactly this kind of reasoning that forms the basis of Mrs. Eddy's philosophy and the entire foundation of Christian Science practice. Sin, sickness and death are equally relegated to these peculiar logical dungeons of Christian Science reasoning processes and then represented as "illusions of Mortal Mind." Regarding this phantom "Mortal Mind" Mrs. Eddy wrote:

At best, matter is only a phenomenon of mortal mind of which evil is the highest degree; but really there is no such thing as mortal mind,—though we are compelled to use the phrase in the endeavor to express the underlying thought (*Unity of Good*, p. 50).

These are strange words indeed, are they not—giving a name to an illusion that does not exist, representing it as evil which is equally non-existent, and then blaming it for all physical woes which cannot exist, since there is no reality or existence apart from Mind, or God? This type of reasoning is considered sound thinking by Christian Scientists the world over; however, the reader is urged to form his own conclusions dictated by the obvious facts that matter is demonstrably "real" and its decay and death are an ever-present problem.

The syllogism—(1) God is all, God is Mind, therefore Mind is all, and (2) Mind is all, matter is not mind, therefore matter has no existence; these are only escape mechanisms from the objective world of material reality to the subjective world of idealism which can never answer the problems of evil, sin, sickness, or material death since they are negated by the assumption that only Mind exists and it is immaterial, therefore not subject to those material categories. By denying even that portion of the mind which recognizes these physical realities, and calling it "Mortal Mind," Mrs. Eddy has forever isolated herself and Christian Science from the realm of objective reality, since the mind that truly rejects the existence of matter must never allow the limitations of matter which constitute physical existence. But in practice no Christian Scientist holds these tenets as an Absolute—they all clothe, feed, and house the illusion of Mortal Mind called their bodies and many go to dentists and surgeons for the filling of imaginary cavities and the setting of non-existent bones. If these facts are not proof positive that the entire philosophy of Christian Science in principle and practice is a huge philosophic hoax, then the authors despair of man's ability to analyze available evidence and arrive at logical conclusions. Even in its basic propositions the Eddy philosophy is a sorry foundation for faith by all honest standards and an almost unbelievable imposition upon the principles of sound logic. So much then for the philosophic theory of Christian Science; let us now examine the theology of this unusual cult, in reality a branch of ancient gnosticism revitalized by Mrs. Eddy's uncanny ability to rephrase an old error of church history and make it palatable to countless thousands under the new guise of Christian Science.

I. INSPIRATION AND AUTHORITY OF THE BIBLE.

Christian Science as a theology and all Christian Scientists, for that matter, both affirm that the Bible is God's Word and quote Mrs. Eddy to "prove" that their whole religion is based upon the teachings of Scripture. Mrs. Eddy said:

> The Bible has been my only authority. I have had no other guide in the 'straight and narrow' way of truth (*Science and Health*, p. 126).

However Mrs. Eddy and Christian Science have repudiated and contradicted this affirmation numerous times (see *Miscellaneous Writings*, pp. 169-170, and *Science and Health*, pp. 517, 537, etc.) and in reality have perverted the clear teachings of the Bible to serve their own ends.

In the Psalm 119 we read: "Forever, O Lord, thy *Word* is settled in heaven . . . thy *Word* is very pure . . . thy *Word* is true from the beginning." The prophet Isaiah reminds us: "The *Word* of our God shall stand for ever" (Isa. 40:8), and Christ Himself confirmed these great truths when He said: "The Scriptures *cannot* be broken . . . Heaven and earth shall pass away but my Word shall never pass away" (John 10:35; Matt. 24:35). It will be remembered also that St. Paul stamped with divine authority the testimony of the Scriptures when he wrote: "All scripture is given by inspiration of God, and is profitable for doctrine, for reproof, for correction, for instruction in righteousness" (II Tim. 3:16).

Coupled with these unassailable voices of testimony as to the Bible's authority, it is evident from the words of Jesus Himself and the writings of His disciples and apostles that He believed in the authority of the Old Testament most emphatically, and even alluded to Old Testament characters and events, thus establishing the authenticity and trustworthiness of the Old Testament.

But this is not the attitude of Mrs. Eddy and Christian Scientists who allege that they believe in Jesus and whatever He taught. Mrs. Eddy herself denied the creation account of Genesis 3 (*Science and Health,* p. 537) and whatever other parts of the Bible did not agree with her preconceived concept of what God, creation, matter, prophecy, etc. should be. She conformed the Bible to her theology, *not* her theology to the Bible. By denying the creation accounts of Moses and the material existence of man, the universe and the origin of evil (Satan), Mrs. Eddy elevated herself to the position of both judge and jury in determining the validity of the Divine Record. Mrs. Eddy, however, had none of the qualifications for this exalted office, being totally ignorant as she was of both the languages and the history of the Old Testament, and completely devoid of any education sufficient to justify her blatant contradictions of the Biblical revelation. Suffice it to say that not one per cent of the Christian Scientists following Mrs. Eddy's system today are qualified to defend from the

Bible their beliefs, since the testimony of Scripture repudiates
and refutes their un-Biblical theology. The Bible declares that
It, not Mrs. Eddy and Christian Science, is the supreme
authority on the activities of God and His relationship to
man. Christian Science employs every art and method of
paradoxical reasoning to escape the dilemma with which it is
faced. It switches terminology about until the terms in question lose all logical meaning (see chart at end of fifth chapter)
and spiritualizes texts until they are literally milked dry of any
Divine revelation whatsoever. To the average Christian Scientist the Bible is a compilation of ancient writings "full of
hundreds of thousands of textual errors . . . its divinity is . . .
uncertain, its inspiration . . . questionable . . . It is made up
of metaphors, allegories, myths and fables . . . It cannot be
read and interpreted literally . . ."[2] Consequently Christian
Scientists believe, owing to the utter and hopeless confusion
that the Bible allegedly engenders without a qualified inter-
preter, that it is necessary to have someone interpret the Bible
for them. Mrs. Eddy is the divinely appointed person to ful-
fill this task. Through *Science and Health,* she, they affirm,
"rediscovered the healing principle of Jesus and his disciples
lost since the early Christian era" and has *blessed the world*
with Christian Science—the "Divine Comforter." To all Christian Scientists then, since they swear allegiance to Mrs. Eddy,
"the material record of the Bible . . . is no more important
to our well-being than the history of Europe and America"
(*Miscellaneous Writings,* p. 170).

The reader is asked to compare this supposedly "Christian"
view with the foregoing Scriptural references and the words
of Christ and St. Paul who said and wrote respectively:

"Sanctify them through thy truth: thy *Word* is truth" (John 17:17).
"But continue thou in the things which thou hast learned and hast
been assured of, knowing of whom thou hast learned them; and that
from a child thou has known the *holy scriptures,* which are able to

[2]I. M. Haldeman, *Christian Science in the Light of Holy Scripture,* p. 377.

make thee wise unto salvation through faith which is in Christ Jesus" (II Tim. 3:14, 15).

God has repeatedly warned us in His Word to beware of those who "preach other gospels" and to be alert to their menace and our responsibility. "But though we, or an angel from heaven, preach any other gospel unto you than that which we have preached unto you, let him be accursed" (Gal. 1:8).

St. Peter also adjures us to guard against "false teachers" who shall bring in "damnable heresies" "even denying the Lord that bought them" (II Pet. 2:1). The time is upon the church of our age when many no longer listen to "sound doctrine" but "gather unto themselves teachers who tickle their ears." Christian Science is one of these false teachers and Mrs. Eddy the purveyor of what Peter so pointedly characterized as "damnable heresies."

Christian Science then is another gospel and in no sense the figure of the true, denying as it does the very core of the Christian faith, God's Word. The inspiration of the Bible is the foundation stone of Christian theology—the authority of the Bible the basis of our hope for redemption to immortality. We are told in the words of St. Peter:

"Knowing this first, that no prophecy of the scripture is of any private interpretation. For the prophecy came not in old time by the will of man: but holy men of God spake as they were moved by the Holy Ghost" (II Pet. 1:20,21).

By these things of course we do not mean that God dictated or mechanically reproduced the Bible, or even that He wrote tangibly, using the hands of men as an adult guides the hand of a child, but that God spoke and caused to be recorded truly and without error those things necessary for our salvation and an understanding of His sovereign purposes and love. The Bible is the inspired, infallible, inerrant Word of God, and is wholly dependable in whatever fields it speaks. This of course holds true only for the original manuscripts of the Bible of which we have excellent reproductions. No scholar to our knowledge, however, holds to the infallibility of copies or translations which sometimes, in minor points only, suggest textual difficulties. The Bible, therefore, stands paramount as God's revelation to man, the simple presentation of infinite values and truths clothed in the figures of time and space. Christian Science, by denying many of these truths and the veracity of the Bible itself in favor of Mrs. Eddy's "interpretations," disobeys directly the injunction of God to "study" and "believe" His Word which alone is able to make us "wise unto salvation through faith in Christ Jesus."

II. The Doctrine of the Trinity and the Deity of Christ.

One prominent trait of all non-Christian religions and cults is their pointed denial of the Scriptural doctrine of the Trinity and the Deity of Jesus Christ. Christian Science ranges high in this category on the basis that it unequivocably denies the true deity of our Lord and the triunity of the Godhead (Col. 2:9). Mrs. Eddy said, and most decisively so, that "the theory of three persons in one God (that is, a personal trinity or triunity) suggests heathen gods, rather than the one ever-present I Am" (*Science and Health,* p. 152). Going beyond this declaration Mrs. Eddy also wrote: "Jesus Christ is not God as Jesus Himself declared but is the son of God" (*Science and Health,* p. 361), and she then crowned this travesty with the astounding "revelation" that "Life, Truth, Love constitute the triune God" (*Science and Health,* pp. 226, 227). Thus it was that with one sweep of a blushing pen a vindictive, ignorant, untrained and egocentric old woman banished God from her religion forever. It is hardly necessary to examine at length the doctrine of the trinity and the deity of Christ to refute Mrs. Eddy's vague ramblings, but it is profitable, we believe, to review those passages of Scripture which so thoroughly unmask the pronounced shallowness of the Christian Science contentions.

In Genesis 1:26 - "Let *us* make man in *our* image, after *our* likeness."

11:7 - "Let *us* go down, and there confound their language."

Isaiah 6:8 - "Who will go for *us?*"

Then we could mention Genesis 18 where Abraham addresses God personally as Lord (Jehovah) over ten times; the obvious plurality of the Godhead is strongly implied if not expressly declared. The fact that God intended to beget a Son after the flesh and of the line of David by virgin birth (Isa. 7:14; 9:6; Mic. 5:2; Matt. 1:23; Luke 1:35; cf. Ps. 2:7 and Heb. 1:5; 5:5 and Acts 13:33), that this Son in the likeness of flesh was His eternal *Word* or *Wisdom* (Prov. 8:22; John 1:1, 14, 18), and that He is true Deity (Col. 2:9; Phil. 2:8-11; Rev. 1:8, 17, 18; Heb. 1:1-4, etc.) and a separate Person from God the Father, is all indicative of the truth that Jesus Christ was truly the God-Man of prophecy and the *personal* Messiah of Israel. It is fruitful to note also that Mrs. Eddy recognizes the "true" God not as Jehovah but as "I Am" (*Science and Health,* p. 152), apparently oblivious of the fact that the word "Jehovah" is itself taken from the Hebrew verb form "to be" (Exod. 3:14), literally "I was, I am, I continue to be" or as the Jews render it "the Eternal"—(YHWH—the tetragrammaton). Keeping with this vein of thought it will be easily recognized that Jesus identified Himself with the same "I Am" or Jehovah—and in fact claimed in no uncertain terms that He was that I Am (John 8:58) for which the Jews were ready to stone Him to death on the grounds of blasphemy (John 8:59 and 10:30-33).

As to Mrs. Eddy's argument that Jesus was God's Son, *not* God, the answer is painfully simple, when thoroughly analyzed. The solution is briefly this: Christ was God's Son by Nature not creation as we are, hence His intrinsic character was that of Deity—His attributes were Divine—He possessed "all power," etc. (Matt. 28:18). He therefore could *not* be a true Son unless He were truly Divine; therefore He could not be the Son of God at all without at once being "God the Son," i.e., of the very Nature of His Father. The Scriptures declare God's Son is Deity—"The mighty God . . . the Everlasting Father, or the Image of God . . . Impress of His Substance . . . Radiance of His glory" . . . etc. Innumerable testimonies as to His divinity are given, far too exhaustive to record here but evidence nonetheless, and beyond disputation. To reduce the Trinity so evident at Christ's baptism ("In the name of the Father and of the Son and of the Holy Spirit," Matt. 28:19) to three of Mrs. Eddy's choice terms, "Life, Truth and Love," and declare all else "suggestive of heathen gods" (*Science and Health*, p. 152) is a prime demonstration of crass indifference to Biblical terminology and historical theology—an emphatic Christian Science attitude instituted by Mrs. Eddy.

St. John tells us that Christ was by His own admission *equal* in Deity to God the Father (John 5:18; cf. Phil. 2:8-11; Col. 2:9; Heb. 1:3), yet inferior in position and form during His earthly ministry (John 14:28) as a man. The Eternal Word voluntarily humbled Himself, became human and subject to our limitations even to the death of the cross, the Bible tells us, but *never* for a moment did He cease to be what by Nature and inheritance He always was and will be, God the Son, Second Person of the Trinity, Eternal Creator and Saviour of the sons of men.

Therefore let us remember most clearly that Christian Science offers a dual Christ, a great man inspired by the "Christ idea" as Mrs. Eddy would have it, one who never really "died" at all for our sins and one of whom she declared: "If there had never existed such a person as the Galilean Prophet it would make no difference to me . . ." (*First Church of Christ, Scientist and Miscellany*, pp. 318-319).

The Scriptures hold forth as a ray of unextinguishable light the Deity of the Lord and the Trinity of God. We must therefore be ever vigilant in our defense of the *personal* Jesus who is our *personal* Saviour, lest the *impersonal* Christ of Christian Science be allowed further opportunity to counterfeit the Christ of the Bible. This counterfeit so widely taught in Christian Science is merely another of the false theories of Mary Baker Eddy that masquerade under the banner of the Christian religion and attempt to subvert "the faith which was once delivered unto the saints" (Jude 3).

III. THE PERSONALITY OF GOD THE FATHER AND THE HOLY SPIRIT.

In Christian Science theology, if it be properly understood, the term "God" is merely a relative one and bears no resemblance whatsoever to the Deity so clearly revealed in the Bible. As has been amply shown (see Chapter V, No. III), Mrs. Eddy interchanges the terms "Life," "Truth," "Love," "Principle," "Mind," "Substance," "Intelligence," "Spirit," "Mother," etc. with that of God; thus Christian Science contends that God is *impersonal,* devoid of any personality at all. Biblically speaking, of course, this is a theological and historical absurdity since the core of Jehovah's uniqueness was His personal nature—I Am—indicative of a reflective and constructive Mind. Jesus repeatedly addressed His Father as a direct object, "I" and "Thou," postulating a logical subject-object relation in intercourse and at least twice the Father answered Him (see Matt. 3:17 and Luke 17:5) establishing His independence of person. This would have been impossible if God were circumscribed by Mrs. Eddy's theology, for only a personality or cognizant ego can think reflectively, carry on conversation and use the personal pronouns "I" or "he," etc. The God of the Old Testament and the New is a personal transcendent Being, not an impersonal spirit or force, and man is created in His image, that of a personal, though finite, being. The higher animals, to whatever degree they "think," are incapable of rationality and, also unlike man, the faculty of "knowing" as Descartes once put it "cogito ergo sum" ("I think, therefore I am.").

But far surpassing this elementary distinction between the God of Christianity and that of Christian Science, is the inescapable fact that the God of the Bible does what only a personality can do and these traits forever separate Him from the pantheistic god of Christian Science which is incapable by definition of performing these things. Briefly, God is described as capable of doing the following things:

1. *God remembers*—"I, even I, am he that blotteth out thy transgressions for mine own sake, and will not *remember* thy sins" (Isa. 43:25; also compare Ps. 79:8; Jer. 31:20; Hos. 8:13, etc.).

2. *God speaks*—"I am the Lord: that is my name: and my glory will I not give to another, neither my praise to graven images" (Isa. 42:8. See also Gen. 1:26; Isa. 43:10-13; 44:6; Matt. 17:5; Heb. 1:1; etc.).

3. *God hears, sees and creates*—
    A. "And God *saw* that the wickedness of man was great in the earth" (Gen. 6:5).
    B. "God *heard* their groaning" (Exod. 2:24), "and the people complained . . . and . . . the Lord *heard* it . . ." (Num. 11:1).
    C. "In the beginning God *created* the heaven and the earth" (Gen. 1:1).

4. *God "knows," i.e., He has a Mind*—
    A. "The Lord knoweth them that are his" (II Tim. 2:19).
    B. "God is greater than our heart, and knoweth all things" (I John 3:20).
    C. "For I *know* the thoughts that I think toward you, saith the Lord . . ." (Jer. 29:11).

5. *God will judge the world—*
   A. "Therefore I will *judge* you . . .saith the Lord God" (Ezek. 18:30).
   B. "Therefore thus saith the Lord God unto them; Behold, I, even I, will *judge* . . ." (Ezek. 34:20).
   C. "For we must all appear before the *judgment* seat of Christ" (II Cor. 5:10).
6. *God is a personal Spirit—*
   A. "God is a *Spirit*: and they that worship him must worship him in spirit and in truth" (John 4:24).
   B. "I am the Almighty God; walk before me, and be thou perfect" (Gen. 17:1).
   C. God's Son is declared to be the "express image of his *person*" (Heb. 1:3), therefore God is a Person.
7. *God has a will—*
   A. "Thy *will* be done in earth, as it is in heaven" (Matt. 6:10).
   B. ". . . prove what is that good, and acceptable, and perfect, *will* of God" (Rom. 12:2).
   C. "He that doeth the *will* of God abideth for ever" (I John 2:17).
   D. "Lo, I come to do thy *will*, O God" (Heb. 10:7, 9).

From this brief resumé of some of God's attributes, the interested reader can doubtless see the vast difference between the God and Father of our Lord Jesus Christ and the "Divine Principle" of Mrs. Eddy's Christian Science. Psychologically speaking, a Principle cannot remember, "Life, Truth and Love" cannot speak audibly, nor can "Substance, Mind or Intelligence" hear, see, create, know, judge, or will. The God of the Bible does these things; the god of Christian Science cannot. It is admitted, of course, that *a* mind or *an* intelligence can do those things, but then Mrs. Eddy does not recognize the existence of personality in the Deity and only *a* personality has *a* mind or *an* intelligence. Mrs. Eddy's god (Principle) cannot

create nor can *it* exert a will because Principle or even *a*
Principle, if you desire, does not possess a will by any logical
definition. The God of Christian Science is therefore an *It*,
a neuter gender—merely a name—incapable of metaphysical
definition or understanding outside of the maze which is Christian Science theology. St. Paul triumphantly reminds us, "I
know whom I have believed, and am persuaded that *he* is able
to keep that which I have committed unto *him* against that
day" (II Tim. 1:12). The true Christian has a personal relationship with his Lord; he prays through Christ and the power
of the Holy Spirit; he asks that it might be given; indeed,
personal contact is the very source of the Christian's life and
spiritual peace. Christian Scientists have no such contact, and
consequently no real spiritual life or peace, only the riddles and
incoherencies of Mrs. Eddy and a basic uncertainty about
good health.

Concerning the doctrine of the Holy Spirit and the attitude of Christian Science toward it, little need be said since
Mrs. Eddy's attitude was so obvious, but at the risk of re-
petition a short review may be profitable. As a matter of course,
Mrs. Eddy denied both the personality and office of the Holy
Spirit and for His exalted ministry substituted "Divine Science"
(*Science and Health*, p. 55). She defined the Holy Spirit
as "Divine Science—the development of Life, Truth and Love"
and further adds, "That influx of Divine Science" (*Science
and Health*, pp. 348 and 579).[3]

To refute such a decided perversion of Scripture and historical theology one need only recall who the writers of the
Bible and Christ Himself considered the Holy Spirit to be
in respect to personality and powers. In the sixteenth chapter
of John's Gospel Jesus instructed His disciples about their

---

[3]Those quotations not found in the standard edition of *Science and Health* on the
pages enumerated here are to be found in the edition of 1895, and also in the
modern editions although on different pages. The authors have used the edition of
1895 primarily because it best reveals some of the vagaries of Mrs. Eddy's early
philosophic evolution.

new ministry and duties and promised them a "Comforter" who would strengthen and guide them after His ascension. To quiet their fears Jesus told them that it was essential to the coming of the Comforter, who issued forth from the Father, that *He* go away. The Lord said:

"If I go not away, the Comforter will *not* come unto you; but if I depart, I will send *him* unto you. And when *he* is come, *he* will reprove the world of sin, and of righteousness, and of judgment" (verses 7 and 8).

It is useful to observe that the Greek text uses the masculine pronoun *"He"* and also *"Him"* for the Holy Spirit and ascribes to Him a *Will* (verse 7) and the power to "convince" the world of "sin, righteousness and judgment" (verse 8). "Divine Science" has not, will not, and cannot do any of these things since it denies the reality of sin, hence excluding the need for righteousness, and teaches in place of judgment the pernicious un-Biblical doctrine of man's *inherent* goodness. The Holy Spirit therefore is a Person with a Will and Divine power to regenerate the soul of man (John 3) and glorify Jesus Christ. It should also be remembered that He does what only a person can do—He teaches us (Luke 12:12), He speaks to us (Acts 13:2), He thinks and makes decisions (Acts 15:28), and He moves us to do the will of God as He has moved holy men of God to serve in the past (II Pet. 1:21). Further than this the Holy Spirit can be lied to (Acts 5:3), He can be grieved (Eph. 4:30), and He is often resisted (Acts 7:51). All of these things denote dealings with a personality, not an impersonal force and certainly not "Divine Science." Beyond these things the Holy Spirit sanctifies and separates us from sin and prays to the Father for us that we might be freed from great temptations (Rom. 8:26).

Certainly these points of evidence disprove the meager attempts of Christian Science to reduce the Third Person of the Trinity to a metaphysical catchword ("Divine Science"), and reveal clearly for all to see the blatant trickery Mrs. Eddy has utilized in attempting to subvert this great Scriptural truth.

IV. THE MIRACLES OF THE VIRGIN BIRTH AND OF CHRIST'S MINISTRY.

The doctrine of the Virgin Birth of Jesus Christ is indissolubly joined with that of the validity of Old Testament prophecy concerning the Messiah of Israel. Isaiah the prophet tells us that "a virgin shall conceive, and bear a son, and shall call his name Immanuel" (7:14), and that this child was to be miraculous in every sense of the word. Indeed, so unique was this child to be that to Him alone of all the sons of men is the name God applied, the "mighty God" to be specific, the"everlasting Father," the "Prince of peace" (9:6). We are told that He shall reign forever (verse 7) and that the zeal of God Himself will bring this to pass. Unfolding further the panorama of Old Testament prophecy we are told that the child in question will be the Son of David (9:7), of royal lineage, and He shall be born in Bethlehem of Judea (Mic. 5:2). Even more remarkable than these rays of light from God, the Scriptures further tell us that He was to be crucified for the sins of Israel and the world (Isa. 53, cf. Daniel 9:26), and that He would rise again to life and come in power to sift the sons of men with eternal judgment (Ps. 22, cf. Zech. 12:10). But these facts are all a matter of history, which Jesus of Nazareth fulfilled to the letter and which only remain to be consummated at His triumphant return as Judge of the world. Both St. Matthew and St. Luke declare the human fulfillment of God's plan in Mary's conception of the Christ-child (Matt. 1:18-25, cf. Luke 1:30-38). Thus the physical existence of Jesus Christ is a biologically established fact. Christian Science vehemently denies this fact and teaches instead that Mary conceived the spiritual idea of God and named *it* Jesus. Denying as she did the reality of the physical universe, this was a strangely logical step for Mrs. Eddy as opposed to her usual contempt for all logical form whatsoever. But be that as it may, all the wanderings of Mrs. Eddy's mind, be they from Dan to Beersheba, can never change the testimony of Old and New Testament Scripture that a demonstrably "real" child was born to Mary, not an "Idea," and this child existed as a concrete physical Being apart from His Divine Nature and is now forever, for our sake, both God and Man in Jesus Christ. The Virgin Birth therefore is a well-supported Biblical doctrine which contradicts most forcibly the false concept Mrs. Eddy has incorporated into the Christian Science religion.

Respecting the miracles performed by Christ during His earthly ministry, Christian Scientists, whether they admit it or not, must logically deny that they were miracles in the first place and discount them as merely "illusions of mortal mind." Mrs. Eddy states that disease, sin, sickness and death are all illusions; they are not "real" since only Mind (God) is real and Mind is spiritual, not material. Therefore following Christian Science theology to its "logical" conclusions—since the "illusion of disease" can only exist in "the illusion called matter," that is itself existent only in the illusion called "mortal mind" which Mrs. Eddy denies exists anyway, there were no miracles at all because there was no corporeal body to be diseased, hence no need of a cure. Mrs. Eddy wrote:

> The sick are not healed merely by declaring there is no sickness, but by *knowing* there is *none* (*Science and Health*, p. 447).

This ridiculous reasoning on the part of Christian Science theology of course presupposes the assumption that there is no evil, since God-Good is *all* that really exists. Unfortunately it places them in the untenable position of having to account for the origin of the *idea* of evil, for even an illusion must have some basis in experience. Notwithstanding the circularity of this Christian Science argument, the Scriptures

send a fresh breath of intellectual honesty into their account
of Christ's true attitude toward disease, its reality and cure.
The Lord Jesus never told the disintegrating leper as Mrs.
Eddy's practitioners would, "You have no disease, it cannot
exist, only God is good and He is all, etc." Rather He recognized the physical decay and by an act of sovereign grace restored the damaged tissue with one short phrase, "I will, be
thou clean." It will be recalled that the leper in question said,
"Lord, if thou wilt, thou canst make me clean" (Matt. 8:2, 3).
Christ's answer included none of Mrs. Eddy's "Divine Science"
or treatments by paid "Quacktitioners'" as they are sometimes
called. He merely restored the form His power had originally
created (Col. 1:16) and destroyed the bacteria responsible
for the disease. Jesus never healed by denying the reality of
the disease He intended to cure. Rather, He affirmed its reality
and glorified God for its cure. It will be recalled that at the
raising of Lazarus (John 11) Christ waited until he was
physically dead beyond question (four days) and then
restored to the function of life every cell of his decaying
body, and glorified God for the victory over man's second
oldest enemy.[4] We should note in this connection that Jesus
did not deny the reality of death, as do Christian Scientists.
He did not consider it "an illusion"; rather He verbally confirmed it: "Lazarus *is dead*" (John 11:14).

Christian Science finds no support for its denial of the
physical miracles of Christ; deny the physical though they
may, they are established facts. Should further proof be desired, however, the reader is urged to consult the following
Biblical references which prove, we believe, that the miracles
of Christ were physical realities, the result of supernatural
intervention on the part of God in behalf of His erring
creatures:

1. Matthew 8:14, 15—the healing of Peter's mother-in-law.

---

[4]Satan occupies the dubious honor of being the first.

2. Matthew 8:26, 27—Christ stills the tempest.

3. Matthew 9:2, 6, 7—Jesus heals the palsied man.

4. Matthew 9:27-30—Christ restores the sight of two blind men.

5. Mark 1:32-34—Jesus heals the sick and casts out devils.

6. John 2:1-11 and John 6:10-14—The miracles of changing water to wine and the feeding of 5,000 people.

❦ Concluding this discussion, it should be noted in reference to John 2:1-11 and 6:10-14 that Christ would hardly have created wine from water or multiplied loaves and fishes to quench the thirst and satisfy the hunger of non-existent bodies or "illusions of mortal mind," to quote Mrs. Eddy. The nature of all Christ's miracles was that of a Divine-human encounter, so to speak, empirically verified physical events, to meet human needs whether hunger, thirst or suffering—not "illusions" as the theology of Christian Science attempts to make the gullible believe.

V. Vicarious Atonement of Christ.

There is no doctrine found within the pages of the Bible that is better supported or substantiated than that of the substitutionary death of Christ for the sins of the world. As far back in the Biblical record as Exodus, Moses wrote of God's symbolic use of blood for purification and sacrifice. It will be recalled that Jehovah delivered the Israelites from Egypt by causing all the firstborn of the nation, including Pharaoh's own son, to fall under the shadow of sudden death (Exod. 12). The Jews were instructed in this instance to sprinkle the blood of the young lamb on the doorposts and lintels of their homes and God promised, "When I see the blood, I will pass over" (Exod. 12:13). The Lord also instituted the animal sacrifices of the Levitical era and expressly stated: ". . . It is the blood that maketh an atonement [covering] for the soul" (Lev. 17:11). Following this typology through into the New Testament, we find that Jesus was called "the Lamb of God, which taketh away the sin of the world" (John 1:29), and further, that His blood shed upon the cross is our atonement or "covering" for sin, even for the sins of all mankind (Matt. 26:28; Rom. 5:6-8; Eph. 1:7; Col. 1:20; etc.).

The believer in Christ, therefore, is saved by grace *alone* through faith in His shed blood and its efficacy for the cleansing of all sin (Rom. 3:25). John, the beloved disciple, reminds us in his powerful epistle, "The blood of Jesus Christ his Son cleanseth us from all sin" (I John 1:7), and Peter no less resoundingly declares, ". . . ye were not redeemed with corruptible things, as silver and gold . . . But with the precious *blood* of Christ, as of a *lamb* without blemish and without spot" (I Pet. 1:18, 19). Indeed, like a crimson cord binding all the Bible into one compact testimony, the trail of blood courses from Genesis to Revelation, testifying from the mouths of unimpeachable witnesses the wondrous story of God's redemptive love. Listen for a moment to the record of Scripture and the picture comes clearly into focus—God loved us and sent His Son to be our Saviour.

"Christ died for the ungodly," Paul triumphantly cries, and "Without shedding of blood there is no remission" (Rom. 5:6; Heb. 9:22); He purchased the church with His own blood (Acts 20:28) Luke informs us, and John adds to the witness by declaring that Christ "washed us from our sins in His own blood" (Rev. 1:5). This was not a pagan sacrifice to placate the wrath of a heathen god's justice as Mrs. Eddy wrote, but a sacrifice offered "through the eternal Spirit" to free the sons of men from the curse of sin, and open the path of salvation by which now we can have "boldness to enter into the holiest by the *blood* of Jesus—a new and living way" to the very throne room of God our Father (Heb. 10:19, 20).

Contrasting this picture of concrete Biblical theology with

the views of Christian Science, no better illustration of Mrs. Eddy's repudiation of this doctrine can be shown than that which comes from her own pen. Said Mrs. Eddy in speaking of the atonement:

The material blood of Jesus was no more efficacious to cleanse from sin when it was shed upon the accursed tree than when it was flowing in his veins . . . (*Science and Health,* p. 330).

According to Mrs. Eddy, then, Jesus, the disciples and apostles, and the early Christian theologians did not understand the meaning of the vicarious atonement, but *she* did and so she wrote —

. . . He atoned for the terrible unreality of a supposed existence apart from God (*No and Yes,* pp. 44-45).
The efficacy of the crucifixion lies in the practical affection and goodness it demonstrated for mankind (*Science and Health,* p. 329).

This is, of course, the opposite of anything the Bible teaches, and when Jesus said, "This is my flesh which I shall give for the life of the world," and "This is my blood shed for many for the remission of sin," Mrs. Eddy would have us believe that He anticipated no sacrifice for man's sin at all but merely martyrdom for "the terrible unreality of a supposed existence apart from God." Further comment on this problem is not deemed necessary in the light of the obvious denial by Christian Science of this historically-accepted Biblical doctrine, so strongly supported by the Scriptures of both Testaments.

VI. The Death, Resurrection and Ascension of Christ.

In our age of advanced medicine we read of many miracles ascribed to the labors of medical science; but all of these advancements, marvelous though they may be, have only delayed the inevitable decay and death of the body and have yet to guarantee us physical immortality. The Scriptures clearly teach us that it is given to all men first death and then the judgment (Heb. 9:27) even as they tell us that our Lord Himself physically died at Calvary (Phil. 2:8). In fact the death of Jesus upon the cross is more thoroughly substantiated from Biblical and secular history than is His birth, which makes it even more difficult to believe that rational persons would deny it; however, Mrs. Eddy and Christian Science do deny it, hence the necessity of refuting their illogical contentions.

Joseph of Arimathaea, it will be remembered, requested the dead body of Jesus from Pontius Pilate (Matt. 27:58) and properly prepared it for burial (verses 59-60) as was the custom of the Jews. One thing that Joseph knew above anything else in the gathering shadows of the Sabbath that marked a solemn hour rent by bitterness, sorrow and fear, was that the body of the Galilean Prophet he buried was physically incapable of life; Jesus of Nazareth was dead. The absolute terror and doubt that gripped the immediate followers of Jesus could have come only from the personal knowledge that He had perished under the Judaeo-Roman conspiracy and that their cause was without a visible leader and apparently doomed to failure. The Apostle Paul tells us repeatedly "Christ died" (Rom. 5:6); Peter recounts that He "bare our sins in his own body on the tree" (I Pet. 2:24), and John testifies that the soldiers "saw" . . . when they came to Jesus . . . "that he was dead already" (John 19:33). Certainly such intimate accounts cannot be lightly dismissed, yet Mrs. Eddy and Christian Science boldly assert "His disciples believed Jesus dead while he was hidden in the sepulchre; whereas he was alive . . ." (*Science and Health*, p. 349), and once again she states:

Jesus' students . . . did not perform any wonderful works until they saw him after his crucifixion and learned that he had *not* died (*Science and Health*, pp. 350-351).

The issue therefore is a clean-cut one. The Bible says Christ died upon the cross; Mrs. Eddy and Christian Science say He did not. For those who call themselves Christians the choice is not a difficult one to make, and for those who are not Christians we are certain they will accept the words of the Scripture in preference to Mrs. Eddy anyhow, if only on general principles and the testimony of history.

The resurrection of Christ is treated on a similar basis by the Christian Science religion which affirms that He never rose from the dead physically any more than He died physically, and Mrs. Eddy deliberately perverted numerous texts of Scripture to glean support for her wobbly propositions. Mrs. Eddy wrote with complete lack of concern for Biblical doctrine:

> To accommodate himself to immature ideas of spiritual power . . . Jesus *called* the body which by this power he raised from the grave, "flesh and bones" (*Science and Health,* p. 209).

So it is that we learn how Christian Science often attempts to change the obvious meaning of texts. In the twentieth chapter of John's Gospel the resurrected Jesus, to prove to the doubting Thomas that He was not a Spirit but genuine "flesh and bones," presented His body bearing the imprint of nails and spear for the disciples' examination. To His disciples at another time Jesus also said, "Handle me, . . . for a spirit hath not flesh and bones, as ye see me have" (Luke 24:39). The resurrection of Christ and its startling revelation —namely, that He was who He claimed to be, the Son of God—is the one factor which most probably accounts for the rapid rise of Christianity's power over the lives of men. Here was a genuine opportunity to believe in a Saviour who proved His Divinity by vanquishing death, and who promised the same victory to those who believe and preach His gospel. It is no wonder Satan has so strenuously opposed this doctrine of Scripture, for upon it hangs the verity of our gospel. As St. Paul puts it, "If Christ be not raised, your faith is vain; ye are yet in your sins" (I Cor. 15:17). Mrs. Eddy and Christian

Science may oppose this truth vigorously, as indeed they do—
but the gospel of Christ will not be hindered by mere denials,
and their unbelief does not in any sense nullify the truth of
God as the Scriptures so powerfully declare it:

> "But now is Christ risen from the dead, and become the firstfruits
> of them that slept. For since by man came death, by man came also the
> resurrection of the dead. For as in Adam all die, even so in Christ
> shall all be made alive"[5] (I Cor. 15:20-22).

As to the doctrine of the ascension of Christ into heaven,
physically, another denial is vouchsafed from the pen of Mrs.
Eddy. By the same method she uses to spiritualize the resurrection of Christ, Mrs. Eddy also spiritualizes His ascension.
She describes it thusly:

> . . . (the disciples') . . . dear Master would rise again in the
> *spiritual scale* of existence and fly beyond their apprehension . . .
> He would disappear to material sense, in that *change* which has since
> been called the ascension (*Science and Health*, p. 339).

Now to any alert Bible student the ascension of Christ
was a physical one; the disciples *saw* Him carried into the
heavenlies visibly; it was not merely an upward stroke on the
"spiritual scale" of existence as Mrs. Eddy put it, but a change
of position from one sphere to another visible in part to the
human eye. In connection with this one need only remember
the testimony of the angels who escorted their Lord to His
throne:

> "Ye men of Galilee, why stand ye gazing up into heaven? this
> same Jesus, which is taken up from you into heaven, shall so come
> in like manner as ye have seen him go into heaven" (Acts 1:11).

Beside these great declarations of Scripture, the confused
writing of Mrs. Eddy is conspicuously immature and inadequate since, as always, the Bible, which is the supreme
Christian authority, confirms the truth as it really happened,
not as Christian Science has imagined it happened.

---

[5]Or to more properly grasp the sense of the Greek, "As in Adam all die, so then
through Christ shall all be resurrected."

VII. THE EXISTENCE OF SATAN, EVIL AND SIN.

Probably one of the most obvious doctrines of Biblical theology is that of the origin, existence and final disposition of evil. From Genesis to Revelation one can distinguish the powers set in array against God and His people, powers whose ultimate end is spiritual judgment of the most terrible order. We are told in the Scripture that Satan or Lucifer, the "god of this world," was once a mighty and perfect son of God whose dazzling and wondrous countenance earned for him the titles, "Son of the Morning" and "Covering Cherub" (Isa. 14:12 and Ezek. 28:14). The Scriptures also tell us that this powerful angel secretly cherished the desire to usurp the throne of his Maker (Isa. 14:13, 14) and upon gathering numerous supporters he rebelled against the sovereignty of Jehovah. The outcome of this wicked rebellion was the driving from heaven of Satan and the fallen angels that followed him, and he was subsequently allowed dominion over the celestial universe for reasons best known to God and himself, hence his title "prince of the powers of the air"—Eph. 2:2).

With this rebellion commenced the beginning of all evil or sin, i.e., that which is opposed to the will of God. After his rout in the heavenly encounter, Satan extended his kingdom over the heavenlies and the earth, determined to disrupt, if possible, the plans of God. In the Garden of Eden Satan's desires reached fruition and he succeeded in spiritually corrupting the future parents of the human race, Adam and Eve (Gen. 3). As punishment for this sin against the Lord, Satan was sentenced to a humiliating defeat by the "Seed" of the very creatures he had so willfully wronged (Gen. 3:15). This promised Seed who would bruise the head of Satan was to be the Messiah of Israel whom we have already seen is the Lord Jesus Christ. The final judgment of Satan will come after his complete and utter defeat at Armageddon, when he and all his followers from the ancient days of his heavenly citizen-

ship will then be cast into the lake of fire (Rev. 20:10), there
to suffer eternally the righteous judgment of God (Rev. 20:10).

Despite this graphic Biblical portrayal of Satan available
for all to see, Mrs. Eddy and Christian Science energetically
deny his existence and refer to him as ". . . another elusive
personification named Satan" (*Science and Health*, p. 81).
Further establishing her contention that evil is non-existent,
Mrs. Eddy flatly states:

> Evil has no reality. It is neither person, place nor thing but is
> simply a belief, an illusion of material sense (*Science and Health*, p. 237).
> There never was a moment in which evil was real (*No and Yes*,
> p. 33).

Since Christian Science denies the origin of evil or Satan,
it is only logical that it should deny evil and sin as the result
of evil. Concerning sin Mrs. Eddy wrote:

> The belief of sin . . . is an unconscious error in the beginning
> (*Science and Health*, p. 81).
> There is no sin. . . . Man is incapable of sin . . . (*Science and
> Health*, Edition of 1917, pp. 447-475).

Placing these declarations on a level plane with the Biblical definition and development of the doctrine of sin, it is seen
to be at complete odds with the Biblical record. St. John
reminds us that sin, far from being an "illusion" or a non-
existent force, is in reality a very potent enemy of man. "Sin,"
writes St. John, "is the transgression of the law," and further,
"All unrighteousness is sin" (I John 3:4 and I John 5:17).
St. Paul also admonishes "for the wages of sin is death"
(Rom. 6:23). One can hardly be expected to believe that the
Christian Science teaching about sin is truthful when both
St. John and St. Paul, inspired spokesmen of God, so clearly
contradict it. The Bible innumerable times declares: "All
have sinned, and come short of the glory of God" (Rom. 3:23),
and "if we say that we have not sinned, we make him [God]
a liar, and his word is not in us" (I John 1:10). As to the
personality and power of a personal force of evil (Satan), the

Bible equally establishes his existence as opposed to Mrs. Eddy's denials. Jesus, it will be remembered, spoke with Satan who tempted Him (Luke 4:3-6). This could hardly have been an illusion even of the Christian Science variety, and the Lord also announced that He had come "to destroy the works of the devil" whom He described as "a liar and a murderer from the beginning who abode not in the truth, a liar and the father of it" (John 8:44). "Mrs. Eddy's devil," as Mr. Wiggin so aptly put it, was Malicious Animal Magnetism which she invented to explain away the rather obvious fact that evil and sin existed despite her affirmations to the contrary. This doctrine eventually became a mania with Mrs. Eddy and drove her to irrational behavior and fantastically absurd demonstrations of temper, illness and rapid excursions to different communities, "when she felt the Fiend closing in."

The Scriptures, therefore, give more than convincing proof "that God will judge sin" and that it is not an illusion but an ever-present enemy which all men and even Christian Scientists must reap the wages of in the end. It is comforting to know from a Biblical standpoint that though "the wages of sin is death . . . the gift of God is eternal life through Jesus Christ our Lord" (Rom. 6:23).

VIII. The Reality and Nature of Heaven and Hell.

God's Word is most explicit in making an unmistakable distinction between those who accept and those who reject the gospel of Jesus Christ. The distinction itself is twofold —that of everlasting life or death to the soul, a direct result of whatever attitude man chooses to entertain toward the Son of God. There can be no middle road of redemption for the souls of men; there is only the narrow way and the straight gate that leads to eternal life, or the broad way which leadeth to destruction (Matt. 7:13).

The Bible irretractably commits itself to a final judgment for all men and a future of either everlasting happiness or retribution, depending upon the decision of man in regard to Christ. The Lord Jesus firmly promised a home eternal in the heavens that fadeth not away (II Cor. 5:1 and I Pet. 1:4), a personal conscious existence with the true God through faith in His sacrifice and resurrection. To those who reject Him Christ promises eternal judgment upon sins unforgiven and the certainty of "outer darkness . . . and gnashing of teeth" (Matt. 25:30). Although Jesus spoke of the Kingdom* of Heaven (Greek—The Heavenly One) as being "within you" (Luke 17:21), never did He teach that it was a "state of mind" or ". . . the reign of Divine Science" as Christian Science teaches. To Christ, His disciples and apostles, heaven was the personal abode of God the Father (Acts 7:49), not an ethereal existence, but a spiritual attainment of close personal fellowship, prior to the reuniting of soul and body at the resurrection of the dead (I Cor. 15).

Mrs. Eddy defined heaven thusly:

Heaven. Harmony; the reign of Spirit, government by Principle . . . the atmosphere of soul (Science and Health, p. 578).

One does not have to progress far in the study of the Bible to realize that this is a far cry from our Lord's description of the coming Kingdom (Luke 17:20), which will usher in the "new heavens and the new earth," the eternal reign of righteousness (Rev. 21). Both the Old and the New Testaments strongly corroborate each other in relation to the visible return of the Lord Jesus Christ and His establishment of a corporeal kingdom—a tangible reality. (See Amos 9:8-15; Zech. 14:4; Ezek. 39:20-28; Matt. 24:23; Rev. 1:7, etc.). In the light of these obvious Biblical references to the existence of the Kingdom of heaven, its final coming and demonstrable reality, the efforts of Mrs. Eddy and Christian Science to explain it away as merely "harmony" or "the atmosphere of soul" fall disappointingly short of Biblical truth. One remembers that

---

*Literally "among you" (Greek); obviously a reference to His fleshly Presence as God's Ambassador.

when Jesus prayed, "Our Father which art in heaven," as part of the Lord's prayer, certainly He never taught that God was in a state of "harmony" as Mrs. Eddy blatantly infers. Rather, He promised instead "great treasure in heaven" for those who followed Him (Luke 18:22) and power to preach the gospel of the heavenly kingdom for the salvation of the earthly. Let us not be misled by the subtle appeals of Christian Science metaphysics, but rather let us remember that most comforting of all Christian truths today—namely, that by faith, and in hope, we are looking for God's Son from heaven, even Jesus, who is delivering us "from the wrath to come" (I Thess. 1:10).

Regarding the existence of hell, a place of spiritual torment where the wicked will remain until the end of the Kingdom Age, Christian Science enters a stout denial. In the writings of Mrs. Eddy many references are made to *hell*, but it is always the hell of Mrs. Eddy's definition, *not* the Bible hell. Wrote Mrs. Eddy:

. . . Hell. Mortal Belief, error . . . sin, sickness, death . . . (*Science and Health*, p. 579).

The sinner makes his own hell by doing evil, and the saint his own heaven by doing right (*Science and Health*, Edition of 1914, p. 266).

. . . Yes, there is a hell. . . . The advanced psychist knows that this hell is mental . . . (*First Church of Christ, Scientist and Miscellany*, p. 160).

From these quotations it is evident for all to see that Mrs. Eddy placed herself and Christian Science in direct contradiction to the Scriptures which teach that hell, far from being a mental state, is indeed a terrifying spiritual reality prepared for those who reject the grace of God as it is in Jesus Christ.

Our Lord Himself warned against the danger of hell numerous times in the New Testament and described it at various times as "the furnace of fire" (Matt. 13:42 and 50), "outer darkness" (Matt. 22:13) and "fire unquenchable" (Luke

---

[6]Those who reject Jesus Christ.

3:17) "where their[6] worm [or suffering] dieth not" (Mark
9:44, 46, 48). Unfortunately hell is often conceived of as being
a place of physical torture in a literal, earthly fire, but such is
not the testimony of the Bible. The Bible teaches us that the
fire of hell is a spiritual "unquenchable fire" not subject to
finite chemical analysis. There is no earthly fire which cannot
be extinguished, but Jesus spoke of "everlasting fire" exceeding
by every point of comparison possible the intensity of chem-
ically-defined flame. The attempts of Christian Science,
therefore, to undercut the Biblical doctrines of hell and
eternal retribution on a supposed material basis are fruitless,
since the doctrines stand supported by every major Biblical
passage dealing with the judgment of God and His intention of
fully punishing sin here and hereafter. Consequently, to assume
for one moment that "we get our hell right here on earth"
and that it is merely ". . . the fire of a guilty conscience . . .,"
as Mrs. Eddy insisted, places her once more in conflict with the
Scriptures and in the precarious position of contradicting the
very words of Jesus Christ Himself who said:

  "Ye serpents, ye generation of vipers, how can ye escape the
damnation of hell?" (Matt. 23:33).

  IX. THE DOCTRINE OF PRAYER AND ETERNAL SALVATION.

  A. The doctrines of prayer and salvation are inseparably
joined in the Scripture with the decree and plan of God to
redeem the fallen race of men. The Bible, in places too
numerous to recount, encourages, instructs and even commands
us to "pray without ceasing" (I Thess. 5:17) that God may
reward our faith in His righteous judgments. The Lord Jesus
often prayed to His Father for strength to meet the physical
rigors of daily life and finally the cross itself (Matt. 26:36).
We remember also at the raising of Lazarus, pictured so
vividly in the eleventh chapter of St. John's Gospel, Jesus
prayed:

  "Father, I thank thee that thou hast heard me. And I knew that
thou hearest me always . . ." (John 11:41, 42),

and that He further instructed us to "pray to thy Father which is in secret; and thy Father which seeth in secret shall reward thee openly" (Matt. 6:6). Above and beyond these elementary examples of Christ's attitude toward prayer, it is a well-established Biblical fact that prayer by definition is a direct personal request to God for His intervention, whether it be for the purpose of healing the sick, raising the dead or simply asking for grace and strength to live our separate lives. The entire context of St. John's seventeenth chapter, for example, is devoted to recording the prayer of Christ for *all* His disciples present and future, that they might be protected from Satan and the powers of darkness during their ministry of gospel truth. Jesus understood only too well the need for personal prayer to God in order to maintain close fellowship with our Father, and it is of this that He reminds us when He said:

"Men ought always to pray, and not to faint" (Luke 18:1).

Prayer to Christian Scientists, however, carries none of the meaning that the Bible so clearly portrays because, as Mrs. Eddy wrote:

"Prayer to a personal God hinders spiritual growth."[7]

We have seen, of course, that the God of the Bible is a Personal Being, not a mere "Principle" as Christian Science contends; therefore it is easy to see why the meaning of prayer to a Christian and a Christian Scientist differs markedly. Mrs. Eddy also wrote concerning prayer:

. . . the danger from audible prayer is that it might lead us into temptation . . . (*Science and Health*, pp. 312-313).

The mere habit of pleading with the Divine Mind as one pleads with a human being, perpetuates the belief in God as humanly circumscribed, an error that impedes spiritual growth (*Science and Health*, Edition of 1917, p. 2).

It is singularly peculiar, in view of these contradictory

[7] I. M. Haldeman, *Christian Science in the Light of Holy Scripture*, p. 268.

claims of Mrs. Eddy, that Jesus addressed His Father as a *personal* Being and commanded us to pray a *personal* prayer, "Our Father which art in heaven, Hallowed be *thy* name. *Thy* kingdom come. *Thy* will be done in earth, as it is in heaven" (Matt. 6:9, 10).

If "Give us this day our daily bread, and forgive us our debts, as we forgive our debtors," etc., is not a plea to God, then, perhaps, Mrs. Eddy's followers can tell us what in the name of reason it is. Mrs. Eddy says, however:

Don't plead with God. God is not influenced by man (*Science and Health*, Edition of 1917, p. 7).

What is more evident from this bold negation of Scripture than the fact that Christian Scientists cannot even logically claim that they pray in the Biblical sense at all, disbelieving as they do the clear definitions the Bible gives of what prayer and communion with God really mean. It was written of the Lord Jesus that prayer was "His constant habit, His unceasing attitude and unwearied occupation"; it is difficult, therefore, to believe that He would urge us to pray in the sure knowledge that it "might lead us into temptation" as Mrs. Eddy implied it did. Moreover, the Lord Jesus prayed audibly, "Lead us *not* into temptation," but Mrs. Eddy says audible prayer itself may lead us into temptation (*Science and Health*, pp. 312, 313). One need look no further for evidence of where she obtained her inspiration—it was obviously supplied by the great Counterfeiter (Gen. 3:4, 5). St. Paul, that noble apostle of personal prayer, instructs us to ". . . let your requests be made known unto God" and to pursue "everything by prayer and supplication with thanksgiving" (Phil. 4:6). Once again the inspired apostle flatly repudiates Mrs. Eddy's unScriptural teachings and those of Christian Science, a fact hardly necessitating further comment upon the subject here. Prayer is the life blood of the Christian's spiritual existence, and personal communion with the personal God our ever-present help in trouble, a relationship no Christian Scientist can ever enjoy since they have never known the God of the Bible or Jesus Christ, both of whom Biblically speaking they and Mrs. Eddy, their "leader," unreservedly deny.

B. The doctrine of eternal salvation is so well documented in the Scripture that we feel sure no major comment at this stage of study is necessary; however, to clarify the doctrine as opposed to Christian Science perversions of it, we shall briefly summarize it here.

Eternal life, the Bible reveals to us, is to be found only in the cross of Christ, that supreme symbol of God's immeasurable love toward a lost and dying world. This life, the Scripture tells us, resides in the Person of His Son, Jesus, "the true God and eternal life" (I John 5:20, and John 17:3; 3:16; 5:24; 6:47; 10:28; 14:6, etc.). The Scriptures further testify that God sent His Son to be the "Saviour of all men, specially of those that believe" (I Tim. 4:10). The Lord Jesus Christ by His sacrifice on Calvary has purchased "eternal redemption" for us promising that if we trust Him fully we shall at length be with Him where He is (John 17:24). God's Word assures us that our Saviour is now at the "right hand of the Majesty on high" (Heb. 1:3), and that some day by His matchless grace, we, too, shall leave this vale of tears, forever free of earthly shackles, to "dwell in the house of the Lord for ever" (Ps. 23:6).

"For by grace are ye saved through faith; and that not of yourselves: it is the gift of God: Not of works, lest any man should boast" (Eph. 2:8, 9).

This, then, is the true, the Christian meaning of salvation, not only freedom from fear, judgment and the uncertainties of this earthly life, but the knowledge of peace *with* God "through the blood of His cross," and justification *before* God by "the power of His resurrection." All these things, accord-

ing to both St. John and St. Peter, are the result of the operation
of God's Holy Spirit in the hearts of men, regenerating, re-
newing, recreating, until eventually in His redeemed own,
the perfect reflection of Christ, God's "express image" (Heb.
1:3), shall shine forth triumphant over Satan, the flesh and
death itself.

"Ye must be born again," said our Lord to Nicodemus
(John 3:3); "having been born again of incorruptible seed,"
writes St. Peter; and St. Paul adds, "Therefore if any man
be in Christ, he is a new creature: old things are passed away;
behold, all things are become new" (II Cor. 5:17). Thus it is
seen that God's salvation is not a reformation of man, but a
regeneration, not just a reorganization of his social habits, but
a literal saving of his spiritual life—a complete deliverance of
the completely lost.

Christian Science, unfortunately, does not hold this view
but teaches instead, as Mrs. Eddy put it, that salvation is *not*
a personal deliverance from *real* sin and wickedness, but
". . . boundless freedom and sinless sense," or, as she further
stated, "Man as God's idea is *already* saved with an everlasting salvation" (*Science and Health*, p. 327).

Christian Science does away altogether with the necessity
of Christ's death on the cross for sin since Mrs. Eddy declared
that:

Final deliverance from error . . . is neither reached through paths
of flowers, nor by pinning one's faith to another's vicarious effort
(Op. cit.).

These are strange words in contrast to what Christ said,
"I am not come to call the righteous, but sinners to repentance"
(Matt. 9:13), and St. Peter's immortal sentence, Christ died
for *our* sins, the just for the *unjust,* to reconcile *us* to God
(I Pet. 3:18). Christian Science offers no eternal life and no
salvation for the soul, denying as it does, sin, and hence the
necessity of redemption from it. But God's Word stands sure
in powerful opposition to the falsehoods of Mrs. Eddy and

Christian Science: "All have sinned, and come short of the glory of God," and "There is none righteous, no, not one" (Rom. 3:23 and 3:10); but, "Believe on the Lord Jesus Christ, and thou shalt be saved" (Acts 16:31). This is God's salvation; this is the message of the Bible; this is eternal life.

X. MAN, HIS SPIRITUAL AND MATERIAL NATURES.

Without fear of contradiction all rational persons will admit the reality of their physical existence. There are three principal reasons for this admission which, briefly stated, are these:

1. Man is capable of perceiving his corporeal form.
2. The demands of the body, such as food, clothing, etc., prove that it has a material existence.
3. The human mind is capable of discerning the difference between concrete and abstract ideas, the body being easily discerned as a concrete proposition.*

In view of these three facts, it is worthwhile to note that Christian Science denies without reservation all physical existence as Mrs. Eddy wrote:

Man is not matter, . . . made up of brains, blood, bones and other material elements . . . man is spiritual and perfect; and because of this he must be so understood in Christian Science . . . (*Science and Health*, p. 471).

Not only did Mrs. Eddy deny the materially verifiable fact that the body exists, but she even went so far as to correct God in His creative office by asserting that "man originated not from dust, materially, but from spirit, spiritually" (*Miscellaneous Writings*, p. 357). At this point in her incoherent ramblings and deplorable mental condition, Mrs. Eddy did the one thing which, by itself devoid of any theological speculation whatsoever, characterizes her system of reasoning as that of a gross philosophic perversion. To deny the reality of matter, philosophically speaking, is to predicate the worst type of absurdity, and Mrs. Eddy was not above such a per-

---

*Capable of empirical verification in this case.

petration. Genesis 2:7 plainly states that "God formed man of
the dust of the ground, and breathed into his nostrils the breath
of life; and man became a living soul." Moses further tells us
that God created the material Eve, using a part of the material
Adam, and David said, "It is he that hath made us, and not
we ourselves" (Ps. 100:3). The Scriptures irrefutably declare
that God created matter (Gen. 1:1), all forms of living or-
ganisms, and finally man himself in the spiritual image and
likeness of his immaterial Father. There is therefore no conceivable ground, logically speaking, for denying that man exists
physically as well as spiritually, and Mrs. Eddy's repeated
attempts to do away with the human body, and for that matter
the material universe itself, is only one more evidence of her
unsound reasoning processes.

In regard to the spiritual nature of man, Christian Science
takes a peculiar attitude, but for once an attitude that is logically consistent when followed through. Since man is totally
spiritual ("the reflection of God" as Christian Science would
have it), and God is perfect and incapable of sin, therefore
man must also be perfect as His reflection and hence incapable
of sin. This is exactly what Mrs. Eddy taught. Witness her
own words:

. . . man is incapable of sin . . . (*Science and Health*, p. 471).
. . . man is the ultimate of perfection and by no means the medium
of imperfection . . . If God is upright and eternal, man as His likeness
is erect in goodness and perpetual in Life, Truth and Love . . . The
spiritual man is that *perfect* and *unfallen* likeness co-existent and co-
eternal with God (*Miscellaneous Writings*, p. 79).
In Science there is no fallen state of being for there is no inverted
image of God . . . (*No and Yes*, p. 26).

The logical mind can only deduce from these statements
that the Biblical account of man's fall from perfection (Gen.
3:6,7) and his definition as a finite being (Psa. 89:48 and I Cor.
15:47) are totally in error and that man *is* God, because if he
coexists with an eternal being (*Miscellaneous Writings*, p. 79),
he himself is eternal. The weakness of this position can easily

be demonstrated by the fact that all material things, including the human body, eventually return to the basic elements of existence, and since God is said to have created all that exists both material and spiritual (John 1:3), therefore man in both his physical and spiritual forms is a creature, a creation not of a coexistent or inherently eternal character.

In conclusion, it is obvious to the intellect of anyone reasonably normal that the identification of man and God by Christian Science on the basis of a spiritual nature is completely erroneous and false, if the Judaeo-Christian viewpoint be accepted as to the identity of the true God. Christian Science, it should be noted, claims that it holds the Christian position, and Christian Scientists violently repudiate any attempts to show that their teachings are the opposite of what Jesus taught; yet in every possible sense of the Biblical record, all things having been considered, there is not the slightest possibility that the theology of Christian Science resembles even vaguely the revelation of the Bible concerning the teachings of Jesus Christ. The soul of man, it is true, is immaterial and was created in the image of God, but the body of man is purely physical in every sense of the word. To deny its reality as does Christian Science and attempt to prove that man is totally spiritual, and spiritually perfect at that, is, to say the least, a flagrant perversion of what Biblical theology plainly portrays. The soul of man wilfully sinned against God in the person of Adam (Isa. 43:27); the souls of all men have forever been in rebellion against Almighty God from that day forward. It is only through the gospel of Jesus Christ that this rebellion is brought into submission and that the sins of man's evil soul are cleansed, and the soul regenerated to eternal life. To deny these facts on a Biblical basis is ridiculous; they are far to obvious. To explain them away as does Christian Science is utterly fruitless for the "word of the Lord endureth forever," and "it is this Word which through the gospel we preach unto you."

CHAPTER VII

CHRISTIAN SCIENCE CENSORSHIP AND PROPAGANDA

One of the most distinguishing characteristics of the Christian Science religion is the fact that it apparently always has money to spend for the suppression of unpleasant material arrayed against its better interests. Despite its relatively small size, the Christian Science Church is a comparatively wealthy business enterprise, and it has not hesitated to use that wealth and the position it has purchased to coerce its antagonists into silence where its "Founder" and her church are concerned. It is a matter of open record that Mrs. Eddy herself forbade the reading of any material opposed to her teachings, so fearful was she that an honest perusal of the facts might deprive her of her hard-won crown and weaken her autocratic empire. Mrs. Eddy wrote in her book, *Retrospection and Introspection*[1]:

I recommend students *not* to read so-called "scientific works" antagonistic to Christian Science which advocate materialistic systems; because such works and words becloud the right sense of Metaphysical Science.

Needless to say, most loyal Scientists even unto today are reluctant to dwell long upon any evidence contrary to that on which they have been weaned by the Christian Science Church. Whatever is said against Mrs. Eddy is to them slanderous and little short of blasphemy. They will believe no evil of her, and all evidence to the contrary, Christian Science is for them mankind's greatest boon since the miracles of Jesus Christ. As the authors have continually reiterated throughout the book, Christian Science is in no sense a

---

[1]Page 78.

Christian religion, or for that matter is it Christian at all where the New Testament is concerned; but instead it is a gigantic business enterprise which doubles as a higher form of mental healing, resulting in their churches and general practitioners garnering millions of dollars each year from the pockets of the faithful. Early in the history of Mrs. Eddy's organization-minded church, she instituted two powerful and central bureaus of business administration: (1) *The Christian Science Board of Lectureship*, (2) *The Committee on Publication*. The duties of both these groups are crystal clear to the trained eyes of any good businessman, and Mrs. Eddy was, whatever else her shortcomings might have been, a superb businesswoman by any estimation. Outlining her reason for creating the Board of Lectureship, Mrs. Eddy wrote that one of its chief duties was "to include in each lecture a true and just reply to public topics condemning Christian Science and to bear testimony to the facts pertaining to the life of the Pastor Emeritus."[2] In other words, Mrs. Eddy ordained a perpetual board of historical and theological apologists whose duty it was to answer all criticisms of her philosophy, and to defend her character whatever the cost. Mrs. Eddy, it may be easily observed, was leaving no stone unturned to insure her continual glorification and the sure defense of her doctrines.

The function of the *Committee on Publication*, Mrs. Eddy's second master stroke of business acumen, can best be described by quoting her own law as to what its duties consisted of. Mrs. Eddy wrote in her *Church Manual*: "It shall be the duty of the Committee on Publication to correct in a Christian manner impositions on the public in regard to Christian Science, injustices done Mrs. Eddy or members of this Church by the daily press, by periodicals or circulated literature of any sort. This Committee on Publication shall

---

[2]*Church Manual*, Article 31, Section 2, p. 93.

be responsible for correcting or having corrected a false news-paper article which has not been replied to by other Scientists, or which has been forwarded to this Committee for the purpose of having him reply to it. If the correction by the Committee on Publication is not promptly published by the periodical in which it is desirable that this correction shall appear, this Committee shall immediately apply for aid to the Committe on Business."[3]

It may be profitably surmised from this rule of Mrs. Eddy that she intended to set up a propaganda system of coercion and censorship which was calculated to suppress any and all unfavorable publicity about either her or her church. And this is exactly what she did. Notice that in her above-quoted law (Article 33) she provides for the failure of the *Committee on Publication* to halt unfavorable publicity by referring it to the *Business Committee*—whose function, according to F. W. Peabody, was coercive censorship. Shrewd businesswoman that she was, Mrs. Eddy realized that news-papers and magazines are essentially profit-yielding ventures and that advertising was the chief source of that profit. It therefore became the duty of the Committee on Business to select a powerful Christian Science advertising client, pre-ferably of the offending newspapers or magazines, whose in-fluence could be brought to bear, resulting in either a retrac-tion or suppression of publicity deemed unfavorable to Mrs. Eddy or her church. Not a few editors, we are told, have had the experience of being pressured by these various Christian Science committees, and due to the wealth and prestige of the "offended" patron, been forced to either retract or lose valuable advertising copy. The result of this growing propa-ganda octopus of the Christian Science Church was the fear of all but the most stalwart editors to take a stand against this Christian Science censorship, consequently the Scientists

[3]Article 33, Section 2, p. 97.

smugly continued their propaganda activities evidently un-
hampered. Through the years any unpleasant mention of
Mrs. Eddy or Christian Science has been curtailed drastically
and she has emerged a portrait of saintly womanhood and
founder of a "new" method of healing where "Divine Science"
and its demonstration are concerned. As has been observed
in previous chapters, this is all a phase of The Eddy Myth
forced upon history in a desperate attempt to suppress the
truth about the entire Christian Science business enterprise
and its founder.

F. W. Peabody, in the superb book, *The Faith, Falsity
and Failure of Christian Science,* corroborates the existence
of this gigantic conspiracy against fair criticism by Christian
Science, by producing irrefutable evidence that all Christian
Science Publication Committees were under instruction from
the powers in Eddyism to suppress by every possible measure,
short of illegal activities, any unfavorable data, regardless of
its truthfulness, that may hinder the aims of Christian Science.
Mr. Peabody wrote:

> But other and more sinister duties than those enumerated in the
> *Manual* are required of and performed by this organization. Sup-
> pression is one of them. They must, if possible, suppress publication
> of harmful facts. For instance: A woman of thirty-five years' suf-
> fering from Bright's disease died in Cleveland, under Christian Science
> treatment, and the "healer" was prosecuted for practicing medicine
> without a license. He was convicted and fined one hundred dollars.
> The testimony at the trial showed that, until five weeks before her
> death, the woman had been under medical treatment consisting mainly
> of diet and regulation of bodily functions with a view to comfort and
> the prolongation of life. With the beginning of Christian Science treat-
> ment, she was advised by her "healer" to eat, and did eat, anything
> she liked, amongst them things deadly to a person afflicted as she was;
> and the regular functioning of the body was completely ignored. The
> consequence was that, during the five weeks of the "healer's" treat-
> ment, which terminated in her death, her bowels were relieved but
> once, and her condition, as a witness testified, was "too horrible to
> describe."

As a result of the activities of the local Christian Science Committee on Publication, no newspaper in Cleveland published any report

of the trial, the testimony or the conviction. Precisely the same thing is done, or attempted, wherever and whenever possible.

Another undeclared duty of this committee is the organization of opposition to every effort made for the enactment of laws for the prevention and spread of contagious disease and the protection of the public health. *In this connection, card indexes are maintained of members of legislative bodies and editors of newspapers. Printed cards are distributed to assistants in every locality with blanks to be filled in showing the name of the legislator or editor, "his religion, his attitude toward Christian Science and protective medical legislation, his politics and the names of his influential friends." All this is a close secret.*

I can furnish much testimony to the effect that it is the further duty of these salaried agents of the Boston church to roundly slander, always anonymously, anyone who dares to stand up in public and tell the unvarnished truth about The Church of St. Bunco and its founder.

Inasmuch as these advertising agents are wholly uninfluenced by considerations of truth or falsity and are furnished ample funds to procure publication of their material, their advantage over an honest critic is evident. They say anything they think will be helpful and are insured the last word.

The Board of Lectureships is composed of men who tour the country to glorify Mrs. Eddy and expound her religio-medical "discoveries." None of them is free to speak his mind. All their lectures are subjected to censorship by the Boston oligarchy and not a word may be changed after the lecture has been duly O.K.'d. No questions may be asked the lecturer. Every Christian Science Church must have a lecture at least once a year and is required to pay the fee, which is left to the discretion of the lecturer, and is at least a hundred dollars. As there is no exposition whatever of Christian Science in the churches of the cult, these lectures are the only instrumentality, outside of Mrs. Eddy's books, through which the public may receive authoritative information.

So violently did Mrs. Eddy hate Mr. Peabody for his frequent denunciation of her entire system and character, that she at one time attempted to bar his pamphlets (*A Complete Exposure of Eddyism or Christian Science*), etc., from the United States mails and threatened boycott of all bookstores carrying his literature. Mr. Peabody described it in his own words thus:

In 1901 I published what I called a *Complete Exposure of Eddyism or Christian Science*, in which I set forth the plain truth regarding Mrs. Eddy in the plainest of terms, specifically accusing her, amongst frauds of many kinds, of repeatedly attempting to cause disease and even death by professed mental powers.

When Mrs. Eddy reached the conclusion that the only way to meet my accusations was, if possible, to suppress them, she summoned the local postmaster to her home and commissioned him to go to Washington and endeavor to procure a ruling of the Post Office Department excluding my pamphlet from the mails. However, on the advise of Samuel J. Elder, then Mrs. Eddy's most trusted legal adviser, the plan was abandoned. Peabody, Mr. Elder urged, would get a lot of free advertising and the Postmaster-General would refuse to rule against his pamphlet. Something better must be thought of, and Mrs. Eddy's fertile brain thought of it.

If the mails could not be closed to me, perhaps the bookstores might; so Mrs. Eddy sat her down and seized a pen and traced these pregnant words: "A member of this church shall not patronize a publishing house or bookstore that has for sale obnoxious literature." Dispatched to her Boston agents, the Directors of the "Mother Church," with instructions to adopt it as a by-law and incorporate it in the *Church Manual* for the guidance of the faithful, it was immediately adopted and as Sec. 12, Article VIII of the *Manual* it stands today.

When it is known that all persons recognized as Christian Scientists must belong to the Boston church and that Mrs. Eddy's laws were made to be obeyed upon penalty of expulsion and outer darkness, and that they are obeyed, it will be seen what a powerful instrument of suppression Sec. 12, Article VIII is. It didn't quite put me out of the bookstores; it took me from the company of the innocuous on the counter and numbered me with the "obnoxious" in the drawer. In any bookstore, in any part of the land, the display of my pamphlet and, later, of my book has invariably resulted in the exhibition of the astonished proprietor of Mrs. Eddy's command, accompanied by the threat of a boycott by every one of the "two million" Christian Scientists so long as the "obnoxious literature" remains on sale. Thereupon, out of sight it goes.

Not only is this true of my anti-Christian Science work, it is true of all writings critical of Christian Science or its founder. The church authorities have thus suppressed some of the most valuable sources of reliable information regarding the Christian Science attack upon the Christian religion and upon sane medical practices. Called Christian and called science, it is the negation of both. Professing absolute knowledge, it denounces education and denies the evidence of the senses. A creation of shreds and patches, it could not live a single day in the light; but, through suppression of the results of honest research, is made to appear religion pure and undefiled. Some such suppressions should be cited.

Examples of attempted Christian Science censorship and

propaganda have not been difficult to find since even one of
the authors has been politely criticized by a local Christian
Science committee on publication. Mr. Clifford C. Johnston
of the New York Committee wrote as follows regarding a lecture which was delivered by Mr. Martin at Shelton College
and subsequently published in the Society's magazine, *The
Examiner:*

> The pamphlet entitled "The Examiner" published by you is both
> revealing and encouraging to those of us who are endeavoring to live
> and practice the teachings of Christ Jesus, because it was such living
> and such practicing of the healing ministry of Christianity that brought
> down upon the early followers of the Master the same opprobrium that
> had greeted the Savior. He was accused of blasphemy by religious
> leaders of his day, just as were his own disciples and the faithful few
> that continued to heal the sick, and even raise the dead for three
> hundred years after the Master's crucifixion and ascension.
>
> For your group, or any other group of religious leaders, or for
> any thinker along religious lines to adjudge Christian Science teachings
> as contrary and even inimical to the life and teaching of the revered
> Master, whom they constantly serve, is not unlike the condemnation
> of Protestants by Catholics, and Catholics by Protestants during years
> notable for their intolerance.
>
> Cordially yours,
> Clifford C. Johnston
> Christian Science Committee on Publication*

Mr. Johnston in his letter to *The Examiner* failed to
answer even one of the points enumerated in the lecture
under discussion, and himself made two glaring errors notable
for their lack of sound knowledge. Briefly, these errors are
as follows: (1) He assumes that Christian Scientists are
practicing and teaching the healing methods Jesus taught,
and are leading lives that compare to the early followers of
Christ. (2) He is amazed that Christian Science should be
called unChristian and its teachings contrary to Christ. He
believes us intolerant persecutors of Christian Science.

Lengthy refutation of these propositions is not attempted
here but a word of comment is expedient. (1) No Christian

*Reprinted from *The Examiner,* by permission.

Scientist who lives is today practicing New Testament doctrine which in any way bears on the method of salvation or healing that Christ taught. The principal point of Christ's ministry was not physical healing but spiritual redemption from sin, and even when He did heal it was not by denying the existence of disease as Christian Science does, but by recognizing it for what it was and restoring again the function of the body. (See Mark 3:5; Matthew 9:27-31; Matthew 8:2-4). (2) Mr. Johnston feels that Christian Science is Christian and we are intolerant for not recognizing it as such. But Christian Science, as has been amply demonstrated (Chapters V and VI), is not Christian at all, but a thoroughly anti-Christian, commercialized religion.

We have invited Christian Scientists many times to discuss publicly or privately these various matters at their leisure. Thus far after five years of vain attempts we have found no desire manifested on their part, so Mr. Johnston can hardly blame us for pursuing our convictions.

To those dubious persons who do not believe that the pressure exerted by Mrs. Eddy's propaganda committees is in force today, we feel obliged to review a most interesting example from the *New York Herald Tribune,* December 12, 1951, concerning Christian Science interference with high school examinations:

The State Board of Regents has omitted all questions on the germ theory of disease from its mid-year high school student biology and scholarship examinations in deference to the teachings of the Christian Science faith.

The report continued:

Similar alterations had been made in the January and June, 1951, biology tests, which contained essay questions on disease that the student could leave out. The coming examinations in January will for the first time omit the question completely.

It should be noted that not only the germ theory of disease was omitted, but that further practical questions regarding

health, hygiene, etc., were also deleted. The *Tribune* article
continued:

> The examination also omitted questions on health measures to
> prevent bacterial disease, care and giving of prescribed medicines and
> simple treatments, prevention of illness in the home, and a list of
> diseases for which a physician should be consulted.

Further than this the *Tribune* in an editorial on the same
subject, December 13, 1951, focused attention on Governor
Dewey's statement when signing the bill, March, 1950, allowing these changes and also the protest registered by the
New York Academy of Medicine. Governor Dewey stated:

> I believe it to be a simple fundamental freedom of religion that
> the State shall compel no child to learn principles clearly contrary
> to the basic tenets of his religious faith.

Commenting on this, the *Herald Tribune* stated:

> Governor Dewey naturally did not foresee that the law might be in-
> terpreted in a directly opposite sense. Now some years later the un-
> fortunate consequences are beginning to appear.

It is clear to see that what was originally intended to be a
simple measure of protection to prevent discrimination against
believers of various faiths had become instead a definite
abuse by a minority of the rights of the majority, and this in
the name of religious freedom.

Following this idea through, the New York Academy of
Medicine[4] issued a release to the press, a statement protesting
this action by the Regents, from which we quote as follows:

> Teachers of the biological sciences report that the application of
> this law creates numerous difficulties. It disrupts the orderly teaching
> of biology and hygiene, the basis of modern sanitation and public
> health. It may prove to be an obstacle to college entrance, not only
> for Christian Scientists, but for all pupils who may be inclined to
> neglect the biological sciences related to public health, because these
> subjects are excluded from examinations. The whole structure of pro-
> tective procedures against smallpox, yellow fever, typhoid, diphtheria
> and many other communicable diseases, and the safeguarding of our
> water and milk as well as other foods rests on well-established facts.

---

[4]December 10, 1951.

Such facts must be known to every school child for proper orientation in natural and social phenomena. Ignorance of the reasons for community action in the field of scientific and public health procedure is a potential source of danger to the community.

In conjunction with this notice given by the *Herald Tribune,* the *Saturday Review of Literature*[5] in a brilliant editorial by Norman Cousins declared:

> The Regents did not merely exempt Christian Scientists from part of an examination. They "exempted" all students imposing on the public at large the standards and strictures of a particular sect. The implications are as startling as they are critical. If the germ theory of disease is to be ruled off examination papers, isn't it only a short step away to rule it out of biology classes altogether? What is to stop the same indiscriminate principles from being used in university education supported in whole or part by public funds? What about medical schools themselves? If the principle is sound for high school students why is it less sound for medical school students? (Page 16).

We can only say that Mr. Cousins met the issue squarely and with a forceful logical approach noted for its clear analysis of the problem at hand. As the *Tribune* said in closing its comments, "This interpretation of the 'Christian Science' Act constituted an encroachment upon the spirit, if not the letter, of the principles of church-state separation that should have aroused more attention than it received."

Further than this, Christian Scientists* in other localities have strenuously objected to fluorine being placed in drinking water for the control of tooth decay, not to mention compulsory innoculation of their children against contagious diseases. However, the issues involved go much deeper as will be seen.

The particular power of Christian Science censorship has been directed over a period of forty-five years at suppressing all evidence that would tend to undermine the myth they

---

[5]December 29, 1951.

*In a letter to the *Herald Tribune,* December 20, 1951, the Christian Science Church maintained that they had been misunderstood, and that they firmly believed in the democratic separation of Church and State, and had only asked that their children be exempted from biological questions dealing with germs, diseases, etc.

have erected around the person of Mrs. Eddy, and they have almost succeeded. In the early 1900's *McClure's Magazine,* a sound periodical of the era, in a series of articles, dissected to the minutest detail through the pen of Georgine Milmine the legend of Christian Science and its founder. The articles were, to say the least, embarrassing, and even the most adamant Christian Scientist from Mrs. Eddy on down stood in mute horror as the stark facts were revealed, bolstered by numerous sworn affidavits from the persons in question. These articles were eventually edited and printed under the title, *The Life of Mary Baker Eddy and the History of Christian Science.* The book had a good sales appeal—too good— for it virtually disappeared after its publication, and copies today are collectors' items. The plates of the book by Miss Milmine were purchased by a loyal supporter of Christian Science who had them destroyed, and the original manuscript is safely filed away where it is still no doubt gathering dust. The *Quimby Manuscripts* traveled almost the same trail to literary darkness as have most of the writings of F. W. Peabody, Mrs. Eddy's perpetual adversary, and Adam Dickey's *Memoirs of Mary Baker Eddy,* a shocking report on the closing years of the intimate daily life of Mrs. Eddy at Chestnut Hill. Edwin Franden Dakin's masterful biography has, however, managed to weather the storm of Christian Science censorship and protests, due largely to the fearlessness of Charles Scribner's Sons, its publishers, who resisted and subsequently triumphed over the most violent wave of propaganda and suppression ever attempted by the Christian Science Church upon a private publisher. So clearly does this case of Christian Science business methods portray the true nature of Mrs. Eddy's church that the authors have elected to review the highlights of the suppression of Scribner's, certain that the true facts of the controversy may be seen and the attempted Christian Science censorship revealed in its correct light.

On November 28, 1928, the manuscript which was to become *Mrs. Eddy, Biography of a Virginal Mind,* by E. F. Dakin, was received by Charles Scribner's Sons, and after careful perusal, accepted for publication. Shortly after the announcement by Scribner's that this powerful biography of Mrs. Eddy was soon to be released (May 1, 1929), Christian Science "censorship committees" went into action. A few days after the announcement, Mr. Orwell B. Towne, chairman of the Christian Science Committee on Publication for New York State, paid Scribner's a cordial visit and after polite inquiries departed, no doubt to draw up the plan of attack. Less than two weeks after the visit, Mr. Towne again called upon Scribner's and was granted an interview with leading executives of the company. Mr. Towne's visit this time, though, was anything but cordial for he took the opportunity to assail Mr. Dakin's forthcoming book as "false and unworthy" and even "hazarded some imputations" contrary to the good character of Mr. Dakin. Mr. Towne, however, upon being pressed by the executives present admitted that he had not seen the book itself and knew absolutely nothing of Mr. Dakin's qualifications personally. It was at this point that the first attempt to "censor" Mr. Dakin's manuscript was made. Said Mr. Towne—"It is a very serious matter to offend several million people . . . I suggest you submit the manuscript to our Committee on Publications so that the reliability of its sources and the accuracy of its data may be checked."[6]

It should be noted regarding this statement that Mr. Towne at no time offered to make available the files of the Christian Science Church to Mr. Dakin that he might have the benefit of much vital evidence bearing on Mrs. Eddy. Scribner's, to their credit, flatly rejected what they described as "an invitation to submit to a Christian Science censorship," and Mr. Dakin's book was published August 16, 1929. Follow-

---

[6]*The Blight That Failed,* Charles Scribners' Sons, London, 1930.

ing the publication of *Mrs. Eddy,* the cagey Mr. Towne voiced his opinions and *public* attitude toward the book. Said Mr. Towne as recorded in the *New York World*:

> I do not see how I can make any statement regarding this book. A cursory examination reveals nothing that has not already appeared in public print.

Concluded the article in the *World*:

> Mr. Towne said that he would make no complaint to publishers and book sellers, that in effect, nothing would be done at all.

Little time need be wasted in describing what effect this book had upon both critics and public—it was a best-seller. As one of the leading critics said summing up his review:

> Mr. Dakin has committed an unforgivable offense against Mrs. Eddy, he has done her justice.[7]

With the widespread publicity attending the book and the completely revealing character of its contents being widely circulated, the Christian Science Church* rallied to the attack and the great campaign of suppression was launched. From all parts of the United States and Canada letters poured into Scribner's from their agents, distributors and book sellers complaining of Christian Science pressure and sales resistance. Book sellers, libraries and every outlet for the disputed work were invaded and threatened by Christian Science pressure groups, publication committees and irate church members who even succeeded in having the book placed on the closed shelves of many public libraries, hence virtually smothering its opportunities for circulation. The tale was always the same, Scribner's began to find out, as reports were sifted from San Francisco, Portland, Atlanta, Winnipeg, Cleveland, Detroit, and even Honolulu. The consensus of reports always read identically:

---

[7] *The New Republic,* Lewis Mumford.

*It has been maintained by the Church that they did not endorse the campaign against the Dakin book which did them much harm. Possibly this is true, but documentation is lacking to establish it fully.

Due to the violent protest of the Christian Science Church in
our city and boycott on our store . . . We have been forced to withdraw the sale on your book. . . . We are the third bookstore in our
city to withdraw the sale of this book.

But the battle was far from over. Some book dealers
were determined not to be coerced by Mrs. Eddy's publicity
hounds and one of them gave Scribners a firm statement to
that effect. Said the statement in part:

. . . we became thoroughly disgusted with Christian Science tactics—so much for freedom of action.

Christian Scientists were not to be denied, however,
and pressing to the attack they began the second phase of the
operation aimed at smothering Mr. Dakin's book.

Concluding that the book sellers had been amply fright-
ened and financially harrassed, the censoring Scientists turned
their heavy artillery on Charles Scribner's Sons personally and
literally avalanched the good publishers with adverse mail on
the Eddy biography. The letters ran from bad to worse, and
did not hesitate to threaten the concern with economic black-
listing. The following are sample lines from these communi-
cations:

There is not one word of truth in the book . . . an erroneous book.
You have published a scurrilous portrait, every line of which is
distorted to make the whole a vulgar caricature.
The book and publisher will be boycotted by all Christian Scientists.

Lest anyone should think that this was a campaign by
individuals alone and did not have the approval of Christian
Science Churches, we reproduce below one of the many
official letters Scribner's received from Christian Science
Churches. This one is from The Third Church of Christ,
Scientist of Kansas City:

Scribner's and Sons, Publishers
New York, New York
Gentlemen:
There is a book on the market entitled *The Biography of a Vir-*

ginal Mind, by Edwin Franden Dakin, which is published by you. We wish to protest the publication of this on the grounds that the information contained in it is neither authentic, reliable nor true, that it is obnoxious to all Christian Scientists and misleading to the general public.

We also wish to state that the *Church Manual* of the First Church of Christ, Scientist, in Boston, Massachusetts, by Mary Baker Eddy, governs every branch Church of Christ, Scientist, throughout the world and we are one of these branches. A by-law in this Manual on Page 44, under marginal heading "Obnoxious Books," reads as follows: "A member of this Church shall not patronize a publishing house or bookstore that has for sale obnoxious books."

We are calling your attention to this feeling that if you understood the circumstances you would not want to be instrumental in putting out a publication which was not true and might be detrimental to you.

> Sincerely yours,
> The Executive Board
> (Signed) (Mrs.) Daisy M. Smayer, Clerk

This blatant attempt at economic blackmail by a Christian Science Church was more than even disinterested parties could bear, and in *The New Republic Magazine* for December 11, 1929, Craig F. Thompson, referring to the aforementioned letter, scathingly attacked the Christian Science publicity crusade in an article entitled "The Christian Science Censorship." Mr. Thompson wrote:

An inspection of that last paragraph is revelatory. The appeal to Scribners is not based on moral or factual issues. The withdrawal is not asked because the book is untrue or obnoxious, but because, if it is not withdrawn, the result might not be happy for Scribners. Another church in the same city, however, was much more forthright: "We will have to desist from patronizing your company unless the book be removed from sale."

This open criticism of Christian Science methods touched off a veritable powder keg of comments on the Christian Science censorship attempts, made by a now vitally interested press. Said the *Christian Advocate* in a powerful editorial January 2, 1930:

The courageous fight of the Scribners' firm to protect itself and the people is praiseworthy. . . . Suppose the Methodists who outnumber the Christian Scientists fifty to one should proclaim a boycott against the book and periodical publishers who habitually defame their church. What a chorus of condemnation would be heard! "Narrow, intolerant, bigoted"—these would be mild epitaphs. Yet the provocation in the Methodist case is far more serious. The only difference is that the Methodists are ready to meet their opponents in the open and fight them with their own weapons . . .

Summing up the opinions of an aroused American press, the Authors' Guild adopted unanimously the following resolution on December 20, 1930:

Resolved: The Authors' Guild of the Authors' League of America heartily commends Charles Scribner's Sons for its courage and appreciation of sound publishing ethics with which it has resisted attempts to suppress publication of *Mrs. Eddy: The Biography of a Virginal Mind*, by Edwin Franden Dakin. In adopting this motion the Guild wishes to make plain that it offers no opinion on any controversy regarding the subject-matter of the book. But since the law provides remedies for false statements by publishers or writers, and since the freedom of our press gives opportunity for stating both sides of any controversy, an organized, extra-legal attempt to prevent free circulation of a book, if allowed to pass unchallenged, would constitute a precedent dangerous to the commonwealth. Universally followed, it would constitute a new tyranny.

Slowly but surely the tide began to turn in favor of Scribner's and Mr. Dakin's book, and "whereas at one time 70 per cent of the book sellers of the country had either stopped selling *Mrs. Eddy* or kept it hidden, the third large printing of the book was at this time almost exhausted."[8]

In an effort to stifle the alarming trend of public opinion against their church, the Christian Science Board of Directors employing its usual wily approach took a last reckless gamble. They drafted one of the clever dialectical announcements Mrs. Eddy was famous for and which she had obviously taught them to utilize as a desperate means of escape from a controversy which had now spelled defeat to their censorship attempt. This gamble took the form of a statement which

---

[8]*The Blight That Failed*, p. 14.

appeared in the *Christian Science Sentinel,* December 23, 1929, and which we here reproduce in its entirety:

Many people are opposed to what they regard as censorship. For one reason, the word "censorship" is often used loosely by people who think vaguely. This reason explains, at least partly, why more than a few people, not all of them actuated by hostility, have criticized Christian Scientists for protesting against objectionable books. The indications are that these critics have not known what Christian Scientists actually do in this regard. These criticisms, however, give us a reason for examining our position, for ourselves and for all who may desire to be *correctly* informed.

The right asserted by Christian Scientists is the right to protest against a publication which *misrepresents* our religion, its founder, or its adherents. In short, we assert the right to defend and protect our religion and persons connected with it from public *misrepresentation.* Surely, there are but few fair thoughtful observers, *correctly* informed, who are disposed to deny or deprecate such a right.

Fair and free observers may, however, say that protesting against an objectionable book is unwise; that the protests will be misconstrued and used to advertise the book; that they will do more harm than good, by exciting curiosity and causing the book to be read. Such counsels as these present a question by themselves; they present a question not of propriety but of wisdom. As such they deserve careful thought, and this they have had. Christian Scientists are convinced, partly by experience, that Mrs. Eddy spoke truly and wisely when she said: "A lie left to itself is not so soon destroyed as it is with the help of truth-telling" (*The First Church of Christ, Scientist and Miscellany,* p. 130). An author and a publisher may have shown a lack of feeling or even positive injuries, but as Christian Scientists we must observe the ethics of our religion in all relations and in every situation. We quote again from our leader's writings (*Retrospection and Introspection,* p. 79): "Meekness and temperance are the jewels of love, set in wisdom. Restrain untempered zeal."*

It must seem fairly obvious to the thoughtful person that this announcement was written with a dual purpose in mind. First, it was calculated to picture Mr. Dakin's book as a "misrepresentation" of Christian Science, Mrs. Eddy and Christian Scientists as a whole; and second, to show that the censorship and boycott were not approved by the officials of the Christian Science Church. Both of these propositions were apparently shattered, however, by the existing facts. To

---

Op. cit., The Blight That Failed.

begin with, Mr. Dakin's book was never officially challenged
or refuted by the Christian Science Church as either libelous
or slanderous within legal jurisdiction. To put it bluntly—they
dared not go into a court of law with Mr. Dakin or Scribner's
because they knew he could prove what he wrote and so
they preferred indirect insults to a hopeless legal action.
Secondly, the inference that official Christian Sciencedom did
not condone suppression and censorship was masterfully
decimated by the *New Republic* in answer to a letter written
by Mr. Towne of the Christian Science Publications Committee in New York. Mr. Towne, after quoting the statement
from the *Sentinel,* declared:

> Protests of individual Christian Scientists may not be properly in-
> terpreted as a boycott or as suppression, and reiteration of assertions
> to the contrary cannot alter that situation. The *protests made in this
> case have been by individuals.*

To this deliberate perversion of the true facts in the issue,
the *New Republic* replied editorially:[9]

> This statement is simply not true. For instance one letter re-
> ceived by Scribners came from a Christian Science Church in Kansas
> City written over the names of the members of the Executive Board,
> and signed by the hand of the Clerk. This letter quoted the *Church
> Manual* of the First Church of Christ, Scientist of Boston which "gov-
> erns every branch throughout the world," to the effect that "a member
> of this church shall not patronize a publishing house or bookstore that
> has for sale obnoxious books." The letter of the Kansas City Church
> added, "We are calling your attention to this, feeling that if you
> understood the circumstances you would not want to be instrumental
> in putting out a publication which was not true and might be detri-
> mental to you." If this is not an official threat of an official boycott,
> we wish Mr. Towne would tell us what it is.

It is impossible to improve upon this clear statement of
the whole controversy, hence Christian Science claims of
tolerance bear a closer scrutiny than they have been given
to this date.

[9]January 15, 1930.

The authors feel sure that this enlightening glimpse of Christian Science pressure methods and censorship attempts will more than justify our previous comments. It is not difficult to understand in the light of these revelations why the Christian Science "religion" is not a Christian theology at all, but a thinly-masked business enterprise employing some of the cleverest publicity methods ever devised in the fertile imaginations of the most mercenary of hucksters. In the words of Dr. Morris Fishbein of the American Medical Association:

Mrs. Eddy has had no successor except the great business organization that is today the Christian Science Church.[10]

---

[10]*Plain Talk*, November 1927, p. 26.

Chapter VIII

The Cures of Christian Science

Probably the greatest attraction of Christian Science which draws many to the religion of Mrs. Eddy is the much-publicized contention that Christian Science possesses miraculous powers of healing.

From the first conception of mental therapy and throughout the ages stretching from the priests of Egypt and the seers of Persia to Franz Mesmer, Dr. Esdaile, P. P. Quimby, Julius Dresser and Mary Baker Eddy, one fact has never been taken lightly by the medical profession, and that is the curative powers of auto-suggestion. It is a well-known fact admitted by all doctors that auto- or "self" suggestion regarding various mental attitudes often improves or even cures assorted symptoms of both the mind and body. Innumerable testimonials from the files of reputable psychologists and psychiatrists bear out beyond reasonable doubt the contention that many of man's illnesses are imaginary, or the result of emotional and nervous tensions in fluctuating intensities. More and more medical science realizes the importance of the mind in its relationship to the body, especially the understanding of what is now called "psychosomatic illness."[1] It is a well-recognized medical truth, for instance, that bronchial asthma, a reputed destroyer of good health, is in many cases the result of taut nerves and emotional upsets sometimes deeply rooted in the patient's past, and that even verified allergies themselves oftentimes yield to psychotherapy and hypnotism. Conclusive proof that hypnotism under proper guidance and control has alleviated and sometimes cured various imaginary

---

[1]From the Greek *Psyche* (soul-mind) and *soma* (body)—the mind affecting the body.

and psychosomatic illnesses, is found in assorted editions of the Journal of the American Medical Association and other specific publications dealing with medical research which are too numerous to quote here. However, recently *Cosmopolitan Magazine*[2] printed an astounding and valuable resumé of the powers of hypnotism in which the following statements appeared:

> You may find it hard to believe that pain can be completely eradicated by hypnosis, but the explanation is scientifically valid. By appeal to the subconscious the doctor is able to erect a wall between the conscious and subconscious. Often in cases of severe pain a surgeon cuts the nerve that relays pain. But blocking the path with "suggestion" achieves a sounder result. . . . Two Australian doctors interned by the Japanese found that hypnosis was an excellent substitute for anesthetics that were unavailable to them. They also discovered that it worked wonders in reducing pain and bleeding after surgery and promoted rapid healing. They described 29 successful major operations all performed with hypnosis in place of drugs. . . . Psychologically one person is not really hypnotized by another, rather—and especially in medical hypnosis—the doctor shows the patient how to hypnotize *himself* into a state of complete relaxation. This then allows the doctor to make suggestions to the patient's subconscious mind. . . . Every doctor deals with illnesses that seemingly have no physical basis yet are very real. Migraine headaches, attacks of asthma, ulcers, allergic reactions, high blood pressure and heart attacks, even when they are rooted in emotional disturbances can cause pain, even death. Such ailments respond remarkably to hypnotic therapy. . . . Dr. R. M. Stein, a New York dentist, reports[3] that in dental surgery anesthesia may be localized in any part of the mouth. It is possible to control salivation and to reduce bleeding. The patient may be placed in any position and gags, mouth props and retentive devices need not be utilized. After extra questions the dentist can reduce post-operative pain by giving the suggestion before arousing the patient.

The article states even further:

> Many obstetricians believe that hypnosis for childbirth provides a wide margin of safety for mother and child. In their book, *Psychosomatic Gynecology*, Doctors William S. Kroeger of Chicago and Solomon C. Freed of Mt. Zion Hospital, San Francisco, point out that the major

---

[2]Ann Cutler, *Cosmopolitan Magazine*, May, 1953.
[3]*Hypnodontics* by Aaron A. Moss.

advantage of hypnotism is that there is no respiratory or circulatory depression in the mother or child. . . . Doctors who use suggestion emphasize that it is not a sure thing. It cannot be used on every patient. Results are not always uniform—or predictable . . . but there is never any danger. In 1848 Dr. Esdaile, working in India, reported that he had used hypnosis in performing 300 major operations and thousands of minor ones. . . . Today thousands of doctors are using it, and medical colleges throughout the nation are teaching the technique. . . . In cases where it is applicable physicians consider it one of the potentially great tools in man's struggle to relieve human misery.

It is fairly simple to observe from this amazing and medically authoritative presentation of facts, that auto-suggestion and self-hypnosis are capable of working veritable miracles of alleviation where pain and suffering are in evidence, and they are strangely devoid of any divine claims based on Mrs. Eddy's private revelation, *Science and Health.* There can be no doubt that the proper mental attitude greatly aids our physical well-being and that the mind decidedly affects various functions of the body, but that the mind produces organic diseases such as cancer, tuberculosis, meningitis, cirrhosis, hardening of the arteries, etc., or that it can cure them once they are fully developed is pure foolishness and the opposite of medical science. Innumerable cemeteries are crowded with Christian Scientists who have attempted to do just that and failed. Naturally scientists and doctors allow at times the possibility of divine intervention through faith, and many verified reports of such healings are recorded; but none of them are in any sense based upon the claim that the disease did not exist in the first place as the alleged recipients of Christian Science healings maintain. It is the firm conviction* of the authors, and one strongly supported by leading medical authorities, that many of the so-called cures of Christian

---

*Quite naturally, some Christian Science cures are genuine, which few deny, but since the religion is pointedly anti-Christian it is obvious that another power is counterfeiting the New Testament testimonies and preaching "another gospel," the direct opposite of God's plan of redemption. These false works, we are told, are a sign of the "last days" of which Jesus warned us (Matt. 7:15-23).

Science are no more than the results of auto-suggestion or self-hypnosis. No rational person can listen to the incessant chattering of a Christian Science practitioner either on the telephone or in the consultation room, to the effect that the mind must "relax," "in quietness and confidence," and thus cast out the error of mortal mind by affirming the allness of God, Principle, etc., without becoming thoroughly convinced that auto-suggestion is being utilized to its uttermost limits.

As a matter of course these conclusions will be challenged most vehemently by all loyal Christian Scientists and especially by those on the publication committees who are well paid to act indignant whenever Mrs. Eddy or her pseudo-Christianity are unmasked. It is because of this anticipated storm of out-raged protests that the authors are prepared to thoroughly document their statements. Both the *Christian Science Journal* and the *Sentinel,* in all their respective issues, devote at least a half-dozen pages to the printing of "testimonies" glorifying Christian Science and Mrs. Eddy for alleged cures received as a result of Christian Science practice. It is also a well-known fact that *Science and Health* contains 84 testimonials within its covers which appear under the title "Fruitage." Many Chris-tian Scientists point proudly to these "examples" of how Christian Science heals, and revel in the testimonies printed in the *Journal, Sentinel,* etc. In view of the importance given these three prime sources of Christian Science healing propa-ganda, the authors feel called upon to reveal some little-known but extremely pertinent facts regarding these sources that all may see the tissue of falsehoods which so cleverly veil the true meaning of Mrs. Eddy's "Fruitage."

In the year 1909 Dr. Stephen Paget, one of England's most eminent authorities, published what is now one of the classic works on Christian Science practices, his masterful book, *The Faith and Works of Christian Science.* In this book Dr. Paget examined some 200 consecutive testimonies of "miraculous" healing taken from the pages of the *Christian*

Science Sentinel. The eminent Doctor then commented on each of these cases and added footnotes showing the absurdity of self-diagnosis. Dr. Paget ended his inquiry by writing to a large number of the "healed" disciples of Christian Science requesting additional facts on their cases. It is unnecessary to mention what the results were, but for purposes of clarification it should be noted that "in no instance did he receive a satisfactory answer" from these "cured" cases, and so after summing up the evidence carefully he concluded with this evaluation:[4]

> The vast majority of these testimonies are not worth the paper on which they are printed. . . . These are not testimonies, but testimonials; every advertisement of a new quack medicine publishes the like of them. . . . What is the good of proclaiming that Christian Science heals diseases which get well of themselves? Time heals them. Here is a girl with a cold in her head: she is healed "through the realization of the omnipresence of Love." Was there ever such an insult offered to the name of Love? . . . Let us apply a fair and mild test to these two hundred cases. Let us show them to any doctor; and let us ask him what he thinks of them. He will laugh at them: he will say, "What is the good of such cases? Why don't they report them properly? Why don't they give details? What do they mean by spinal trouble, and all the other troubles?"

In his book Dr. Paget also listed 68 cases of "cures" allegedly received from the practice of Christian Science principles "which were shown to be unfounded and worse by physicians who sent them to Dr. Paget for the book." Wrote Dr. Paget commenting on these cases:

> They display (1) the great liking which Christian Science has for the very worst sort of "surgical cases"; (2) the cruelty or brutality which naturally goes with her terror of pain and of death; (3) the element of madness which is in her faith; (4) the vanity or self-conceit which approves and adopts an illegitimate philosophy, not merely for its own sake, but for the sake of opposition to authority.

Space will not allow a full reproduction of these terrible tragedies of Christian Science malpractice but we here quote

[4]James H. Snowden, *The Truth About Christian Science*, pp. 240-241.

the two cases which came from American doctors, one from a physician in Mrs. Eddy's own stronghold, Boston:[5]

I am sending you the following two cases where the patients were treated by Christian Science, and were worse, and died after the treatment; and the third case, one of "miraculous conception." The first was a man in middle life, who had a mild attack of nephritis, and was told by a Christian Science healer to eat and drink as he pleased, and to go ahead with his business, for "he only thought he was sick." He soon developed uraemic convulsions, and died. The second was a man with a small epithelioma of the tongue, who was told by a Christian Scientist that it didn't amount to anything, and that their treatment would soon make it disappear. He died of its ravages while receiving treatment from them. The third case which came to my knowledge, was one of conception, and the delivery of a child at term, in a Christian Scientist, who declared she conceived by thought, as taught in their creed, and that no man entered into the case.

Boston is a hotbed of Christian Science, and we see a great many patients who are treated by those who practice it. I have seen a patient dying of strangulated hernia, who had been treated from first to last by Christian Science. I should say I had seen about a hundred cases, in which the only chance for cure had been lost through Christian Science treatment.

Surely the unbiased reader can see from these verifiable truths that the claims of Christian Science are hollow at best, and at their worst deplorable perversions when used to bolster up Mrs. Eddy's sagging philosophy.

Dr. J. M. Buckley, noted American medical expert, added his voice to the already rising tide of undeniable facts when at the turn of the century he wrote:[6]

The failures of Christian Science are innumerable. Twenty years ago I collected vital statistics of various communistic institutions which refuse medical aid, and compared them with the tables of life insurance companies; and on the basis of the results of the comparison, I predicted that, should Christian Science at any time begin to spread rapidly, or should anti-medicine faith-healing institutions be largely increased, the number of deaths would attract attention, and public indignation be excited by failures to heal maladies which ordinarily yield to medical or surgical treatment. This prediction is

[5]*Ibid.*, pp. 242-243.
[6]Dr. J. M. Buckley, *North American Review*, July, 1901.

now being fulfilled every day. Many who have been vainly treated by Christian Scientists are now dead. None of their failures is mentioned by the healers, and few of the living victims, who are usually silenced by shame. One I met in an insane asylum, muttering all day long, "God can never be sick."

Christian Scientists, whether they be Teachers, Practitioners, Readers or church members, cannot consciously deny these awful testimonies to the failure of Christian Science to heal, for the evidence is far too overwhelming and conclusive. However, let us return to the findings of Dr. Paget. Terminating his medical indictment of Mrs. Eddy's healing claims, Dr. Paget condensed his opinion of Christian Science and its assorted propaganda efforts into a brief page, noted for its pointed analysis and challenging conclusions. Dr Paget stated:[7]

These short notes, put here as I got them, give but a faint sense of the ill working of Christian Science. It would be easy to collect hundreds more. Of course, to see the full iniquity of these cases, the reader should be a doctor. But everybody, doctor or not, can feel the cruelty, born of fear of pain, in some of these Scientists—the downright madness threatening not a few of them, and the appalling self-will. They bully dying women, and let babies die in pain; let cases of paralysis tumble about and hurt themselves; rob the epileptic of their bromide, the syphilitic of their iodide, the angina cases of their amyl nitrite, the heart cases of their digitalis; let appendicitis go on to septic peritonitis, gastric ulcer to perforation of the stomach, nephritis to uraemic convulsions, and strangulated hernia to the *miserere mei* of gangrene; watch, day after day, while a man or a woman bleeds to death; compel those who should be kept still to take exercise; and withhold from all cases of cancer all hope of cure. To these works of the Devil they bring their one gift, wilful and complete ignorance; and their "nursing" would be a farce, if it were not a tragedy. Such is the way of Christian Science, face to face, as she loves to be, with bad cases of organic disease. . . . In a rage, Commonsense cries, ". . . Leave the children alone. It doesn't matter with grown-up people; they can believe what they like about Good and Evil, and germs, and things. But the children; they take their children to these services. Why can't they leave the children out of it?" . . . The corner stone of her church is not Jesus Christ but her own vanity. She is cruel to babies and young children; she is worse than close-

[7]James H. Snowden, *The Truth About Christian Science*, pp. 243-244.

fisted over her money; she despises Christianity, and is at open war
with experience and common sense. . . . We examine her testimonials,
and find them worthless. We are told that she is Christ come again,
and we can see that she is not. We listen to her philosophical talk,
and observe that she is illiterate, and ignorant of the rudiments of
logic. We admit, and are glad, that she has enabled thousands of
nervous persons to leave off worrying, and has cured many "functional disorders"; but she has done that, not by revelation, but by
suggestion. The healed, whom she incessantly advertises, are but few,
compared with them that are whole . . . and a thousand brave and
quiet lives, the unnamed legion of good non-Scientists. They bear,
not deny, pain, they confess, not confuse, the reality of sin; they face,
not outface, death.

Certainly any thinking person will agree with Dr. Paget's
conclusions since the failures of Christian Science are
numerous, and of common knowledge. Every dead Christian
Scientist is a testimony to the failure of Mrs. Eddy's system
which denies the very reality of physical death itself. Let us
continue with the presentation of evidence.

Professor Richard C. Cabot, M.D. of the Harvard Medical
School, in his enlightening article, "One Hundred Christian
Science Cures,"[8] shows how palpably weak and absurd are
the testimonies offered in support of the Eddy Healing Myth.
Dr. Cabot took his one hundred cases from the pages of the
Christian Science Journal and had this to say about their
genuine worth:

Seventy-two cases were functional, seven were cases of what
appeared to be organic, eleven were cases very difficult to class, and
ten were cases regarding which no reasonable conjecture can be made.

Dr. Cabot concluded that most Christian Science cures were
probably genuine but that they were not cures of properly
diagnosed organic diseases. Far from believing that the
methods of Christian Science are "miraculous," Dr. Cabot
logically shows that they are nothing more than standard
medical procedures. Dr. Cabot said:

Of the classical methods of psychotherapeutics, namely, explanation,
education, psychoanalysis, encouragement, suggestion, rest cure and

[8]*McClure's Magazine,* August, 1908.

work cure, the Christian Scientists used chiefly suggestion, education and work cure, though each of these methods is colored and shaped by the peculiar doctrines of the sect.

It may be fairly observed, therefore, by any open-minded person that there is no miraculous element in the methods of mental suggestion utilized by Christian Science practitioners who employ the commonest of psychological tools and masquerade them and their effects under what is termed "demonstration" and "healing" through the alleged revelation of Mrs. Eddy. These same results sometimes obtained by Christian Science practitioners in alleviating psychosomatic symptoms, have been and are being equalled and far surpassed by properly-trained and educated members of the capable medical profession. There can be no room for those who make merchandise of the truly sick and delude them into believing that what is really serious organic disease, is merely an "illusion of mortal mind," a figment of erroneous spiritual disharmony. This every Christian Science practitioner is guilty of, and how many persons have gone to their grave through the machinations of Mrs. Eddy's* unqualified practitioners, sometimes rather unceremoniously referred to as "quacks" by informed sources, only God and the coroner know. There is no excuse for the wilful neglect of sick children who have often perished through the blind ignorance of their parents, believing as they did the monstrous prevarication that Christian Science is the key to everlasting health. What type of mind is it that can repeat day in and day out to hopeless victims of paralysis, cancer and other biological destroyers the unspeakable falsehood that they are not suffering or incapacitated since "the reflection of the Divine mind cannot be sick." Surely such minds and the souls that govern them find their inspiration, incubation, and development, not in the Christ of Calvary, but in the "enemy of all righteousness."

As to the "testimonies" in the chapter "Fruitage" (*Science*

---

*i.e., To properly diagnose and treat organic diseases.

and Health, pages 600-700) they deserve no especial consideration whatever. Dr. Charles E. Humiston, previously referred
to, exhaustively examined each of the 84 accounts of Christian
Science healings as found in Chapter XVIII of *Science and
Health* and evaluated them from a medical standpoint. It
is the expert opinion of Dr. Humiston that not one of these
"miracles" would have failed to respond to proper diet and
the human body's general ability to repair itself and destroy
invading bacilli. Dr. Humiston challenges the diagnosis of
serious internal disorders such as cancer, tuberculosis, etc.
(pages 610, 623, 626, 641, 649, 666), since no medical diagnosis
was forthcoming other than the patient's word which as has
been shown, in the instance of neurotic and psychosomatic
cases, to be most undependable. In summation of his thorough
exposé of the Christian Science testimony "evidence," Dr.
Humiston said:[9]

> It will be rightly seen that "Fruitage" at full face value is far
> from convincing proof that Christian Science does any better than the
> "ordinary" doctor whom Mrs. Eddy so roundly berates.
> If due allowance is made for such mistakes as are inevitable when
> laymen undertake the diagnosis of their own ailments, Christian Science
> at once appears at its true value as a system of healing, namely, the
> value of the powers of resistance to disease which the body naturally
> possesses. Again, if allowance is made for the part that physicians
> probably played in the management of many of the cases, and for
> the misrepresentation of what the "best" physicians and great "spe-
> cialists" really did say of the cases reported "given up," "Fruitage" loses
> all right to be called "evidence" and sinks to its proper level—that
> of a collection of carefully-edited patent nostrum testimonials.

To further clarify the record where many of the alleged
cures of Christian Science are concerned, the authors here
include a choice selection of thoroughly-documented cases of
Christian Science malpractice and failure which for downright brutality and senseless neglect have no equal in the
annals of man's inhumanity to his own kind. These authentic

[9]Charles E. Humiston, *The Faith, The Falsity, The Failure of Christian Science,*
p. 335.

case histories were compiled by the late Charles E. Humiston, M.D.Sc.D., former Professor of Surgery, College of Medicine of the University of Illinois, an outstanding doctor and an unimpeachable authority. Should any person doubt their authenticity the authors stand prepared to exhaustively prove their reliability along with some three dozen other cases of such nauseating description that they shall be withheld in the interest of proper scholastic presentation. From these examples it can be clearly seen by even the most prejudiced eye that the fruit of Mrs. Eddy's "Science" is far from sweet, for to innumerable thousands it has brought only the bitter taste of needless suffering and death.[10]

CASE HISTORIES

Cancer of the Breast—Fatal.

A woman, aged 42, the mother of three children, in age ranging from about eleven down to three, gave the following history: In June, 1920, she noticed a lump in her left breast which, continuing to increase in size, led her, in August, two months later, to consult Drs. T. and H., who made a diagnosis of probable malignancy. The patient's sister, an adherent of the Christian Science faith, persuaded her to rely on Christian Science rather than follow the advice of the physicians, who urged operation. Accordingly, the patient buoyed up by the promise of certain cure without operation, began taking treatments of a practitioner named Mrs. H.

The patient visited the practitioner once a week to receive treatment, and incidentally to make payment of the weekly charge of five dollars. During the rest of the week absent treatments were given. These treatments were continued until the patient was too weak to visit the practitioner, who lived a dozen miles away. Furthermore, the practitioner requested the patient to take treatment from some one else, as mortal mind was interfering with the case and she could do no more.

Conditions becoming alarming, the husband insisted on calling in a surgeon. On February 14, 1923, I was called to the home to "arrange for the operation" previously advised by Drs. T. & H. Upon entering the room where the patient lay reclining on a couch, she arose and literally staggered as she advanced to greet me. I shall never forget the picture presented in this poor woman's home—poor

[10]*Ibid.*, pp. 338-402. Selected cases.

in a double sense. The patient, yellow as a lemon, so short of breath that her voice was scarcely audible, said that she thought everything was coming along all right, but to please her husband she had decided to withdraw her opposition to surgical treatment, and wished me to make the necessary arrangements for immediate operation.

A brief examination showed an emaciated woman, who appeared many years older than the age given. Her skin was intensely jaundiced from secondary cancerous involvement of the liver, and it was evident that dissolution was near at hand. In reply to the patient's question as to how soon she could have the operation, I replied that I did not advise operation.

In the adjoining room the older of the little children, a girl of perhaps ten or eleven, was attempting to prepare a belated breakfast for the three little ones. On every hand was evidence that the mother had been compelled to give up her household duties. As I looked upon this little family, my professional side gave place to that of the father, for I have little ones of my own. The impending tragedy about to destroy the happiness of this humble home and to despoil this little group of the mother's guiding hand, to me was a situation most tragic. I asked the husband and father to step outside in order that I might tell him privately that an operation would be worse than useless. The poor woman's suffering lasted just two weeks longer, when she "passed on," as her sister informed me—the same sister whose pernicious advice was responsible for this untimely death.

Diphtheria—No Antitoxin—Death.

Several years ago, a woman came to my office and asked me to accompany her to a little cottage in the neighborhood. We were met by the father and mother of a little girl whom I was asked to examine. The little patient, ten or eleven years of age, presented a strikingly beautiful picture as she lay in her little bed with her hair fallen in tangled golden ringlets over her shoulders and upon her pillow. As I approached the bed, I could see that she was not breathing, and on closer examination, found she was dead.

I informed the parents that the child was dead, whereupon they contradicted me, saying: "She is not dead, but has passed on." I asked why they had sent for me, and they replied: "Only to conform to the rules of the Health Department which require a death certificate."

They said that they knew that the child was not dead; that the Lord had called the child home where they would meet her in the future as the child they loved and where she would always be a child to them.

There was not a tear in the eyes of either parent. I asked them what the child had been complaining of, and how long she had been sick. They replied that she had not been sick at all, but in her childish ignorance and innocence, she thought that she had a sore throat for almost a week.

I asked them to give me a spoon with which to depress the tongue so that I could examine the throat. This they did, and, as I expected, I found a diphtheritic membrane covering the tonsils, pharynx, and palate.

I told them that the child had died of diphtheria, and could have been saved by a single dose of antitoxin, had they called a doctor a few days before. This they disputed; and they seemed perfectly satisfied that the child had "passed on."

I refused to sign the death certificate, and made this a coroner's case, where it stands as a matter of record in the coroner's office in this city.

Mental Obstetrics—Fatal Postpartum Hemorrhage.

My attention is attracted to your study of the question of the dangers of relying on Christian Science in cases of serious disease. I am sending you an account of my worst case.

The subject of this sketch of Christian Science malpractice was a Mrs. B., a strong, rugged woman, already the mother of *two* healthy children. I had seen this woman about town frequently and was aware that the number of children in her household was soon to be augmented. I also knew the family to be Christian Scientists. At four o'clock one morning, this woman's husband called me to come down quickly and bring instruments.

I hastened to the "B" residence and was met at the door by a woman in nurse's costume, who conducted me to the bed chamber. Mrs. B. stated that she was feeling "all right" and that nothing had happened. Her appearance belied her assertions. Her face was ghostly white and she was pulseless at the wrist. A baby had been born, but the room and bed were clean and tidy and betrayed no visible sign of any untoward condition. The patient, however, was exsanguinated. It was perfectly evident that she had suffered a dangerous, if not fatal hemorrhage. She was no longer bleeding; she no longer had blood enough to sustain hemorrhage.

Seeing death written in her face, I summoned Dr. R., living two blocks away, and while he was coming, I hastened to the hospital, a distance of one block, for a blood transfusion outfit. Dr. R. answered my urgent call for assistance so promptly that I found him waiting when I returned to the house. The patient was already dead upon Dr. R.'s arrival. The husband and the nurse both denied that there had been any hemorrhage, but Dr. R. and myself could not credit their statements, and agreed that the woman came to her death through loss of blood. Later, the patient's aunt, who is not "in science," divulged the fact that the husband, before calling for help, had burned the blood-soaked bedding, and that there had been enough of it to fill the furnace a second time.

I refused to sign a death certificate. The husband, backed up by an attorney, endeavoured to coerce me into sparing the family and the Christian Scientists the odium of a coroner's inquest. In spite of their cajolery and their threats, I stood my ground. I told them that they were this woman's executioners, that in this day and age, with so many safeguards available to avert disaster on occasions like this, it grieved me greatly to witness the taking of human life through such crass ignorance, and that I greatly regretted that the little hurt to their business incidental to a coroner's inquest was all that a criminally inadequate law could do. The coroner held his inquest, and furnished the certificate, assigning as the cause of death, "postpartum hemorrhage."

Tuberculosis—Hemorrhage—Death.

Last August I received a call to Mr. K.'s house, and found that he had suffered a severe hemorrhage from the lungs. I had previously examined his sputum and found tubercle bacilli. The young man was rejected in the draft. A year ago he started a bakery and was the chief baker. From the standpoint of the public this was an unsanitary proposition. He worked long hours and his vital strength was greatly diminished.

The last time I saw this young man alive was on the eighth day of September. At that time he expressed a strong desire to get back to his business. I told him that such a thing was extremely inadvisable. The time set for him to remain quiet in bed was from six to nine weeks from the date of his hemorrhage. It was plain to me that my advice was contrary to the wishes of the patient. The next day a Christian Science practitioner was called. The patient was promptly told that there was not the least danger in getting out of bed and attending to his business at once. Three days later, I was called to the telephone by a local undertaker, who asked me to sign a death certificate for Mr. K. The undertaker informed me that a Christian Science practitioner had been installed as advisor to the patient and had advised the patient to get up and around without fear of any consequences. The patient had followed the practitioner's advice. The exertion of getting up had brought on an alarming hemorrhage which ended in the patient's death within a few minutes. I signed the death certificate. The name of the miserable fanatic who treated my hemoptysis case to death is carried on the list of those given approval by the Christian Science officials as published in *The Christian Science Journal.*

Pneumonia in a Child.

Just twenty years ago we lived next door to a family of Christian Scientists. The husband and father had recently died of typhoid fever, leaving a family of children, the younger ones being Janet, aged three, and Esther, who was five. Late in the fall, Esther was taken sick with a severe cold. She drooped about the house, coughed, and complained of a pain in her side.

A Christian Science practitioner was employed—a Mrs. B., who came to the house every day to give treatments. The healer would sit in the presence of the child and quote from *Science and Health*. Many times she would repeat: "I can see your father now, he was about to embrace Christian Science just before he passed on, and had he done so, he would be with his little girl today." Esther was encouraged, and wishing to please her mother, frequently asserted that she was not sick. I asked the mother why she did not put some oil on the little lips and nose, as they were so sore and angry-looking. The mother replied, "I am afraid that God would desert us if I used a material remedy." I told her that I read and followed the Bible, too, and that the Saviour anointed with oil. She said, "I wish I had your faith, but I'm afraid." The little child was trying to appear well. While I was calling, she stood in the open doorway in the chill wind and coughed so that it made my heart bleed to look at her. After a few minutes, little Esther came to her mother's side and, half whispering, said, "I feel better, mamma, won't you let me sit in your lap a little while?" The mother said, "Run along, dear, and play with baby sister, I am talking to Mrs. C."

The following day, an older brother came into our yard. I asked him about Esther. He said that the lady healer was in the house then and that he had just overheard her tell his mother that Esther was doing fine, that the only thing to fear now was the opposition of the neighbours. The boy's quivering chin, his worried and anxious look, told me a different story. He came on into the house. I encouraged him to get their former family physician, who had always called Esther his "best little girl." As the doctor entered the house, the mother, in great surprise, said, "Who sent for you?" His answer was, "Where's Esther?" and strode upstairs. In a little while he came down again looking very serious. He said to the disturbed mother, "Esther has pneumonia; she is nearing the crisis, and I'm afraid my 'best little girl' is slipping away."

The doctor refused to leave the house. Toward midnight the little sufferer seemed easier, but oh, so pale. Calling feebly to her doctor friend, who was already as close to her bed as he could get, she said, "I'm going to sleep now, Doctor, good night, I'll see you in the morning." But for little Esther the morning came that night. This tragedy so affected the mother that she made me a sort of health guardian for the baby, and ever afterward, when Janet seemed indisposed, she was sent to me.

Scarlet Fever—Kidney Complication—Death.

In the fall of 1914 I was asked, one evening, to see a three-year-old boy, the child of people theretofore strangers to me, who told me that the child had been refusing food and vomiting for three or four days. He had, that evening, become unconscious. No physician, it was claimed, had seen him.

The child was characteristically desquamating about hands and feet and the face and limbs were markedly edematous. He died the following day and, although I reported scarlet fever and signed the death certificate on the same day, nobody asked any questions. I did not learn until afterward that both parents were "pious" Eddyites.

Pneumonia—Tetanus—Lockjaw—Two Cases.

In 1908, I was requested by the supervisors of our township to go and see a Miss S., who had been reported sick, and who had been under the care of "Scientists" for some time. I was asked to ascertain whether or not it would be safe and proper to remove her to the hospital, twenty miles away. On examination I found a thin, frail woman, quite ill. Her pulse and temperature were high, and she presented the signs and symptoms of pneumonia, but as is not infrequently the case in this very fatal disease, the patient was able to walk about the room. The treatment this case of pneumonia had had could well be summed up in two words—"forget it." I advised against moving the patient, feeling that a twenty-mile ride was out of the question.

Following my report, the supervisor went out to the house where the patient roomed to make some arrangements for taking care of her. Upon his arrival he learned that the practitioners, with two other members of the church, had taken her away. It was brought out at the inquest that they had dressed her and made her walk five blocks in a foot of snow, and with the mercury in the neighbourhood of zero. Autopsy showed well developed lobar pneumonia in both lungs.

We have had two deaths from tetanus following nail wounds in the last twenty years. Both cases were treated by "Scientists" until the disease was well established, when, of course, the time for anti-tetanic serum to be of greatest service is past.

Mastoid Abscess—Meningitis—Fatal.

A Christian Science nurse, by the name of P...., sent for me to "diagnose" a case. The "case" was that of a little girl eight years of age who had been troubled with a "running ear" for several weeks. Several attacks of earache ending in a "gathering" in her ear had been "healed" by Christian Science. This attack, however, was not following the beaten path to harmony. The ear refused to break as usual, and the "nurse," still possessing a little remnant of human sympathy, was distressed to see the "little thing suffer so."

My visit was made in the evening, and I was asked not to let the child know that I was a doctor. I found the little patient in a dimly-lighted room with everybody going about on tip-toe, and carrying on conversation in whispers. The child cried out upon the least disturbance. The condition was plainly that of mastoid abscess complicating middle ear disease. I urged the parents to have an operation done that very night. They said they would think it over and let me know. Near midnight of the same evening the father telephoned me that they had decided to continue the "same treatment," that is, treatment by a Christian Science practitioner.

Seven days later, an undertaker came to my office to secure a death certificate for the little child. From him I learned the subsequent history of the case. There had been delirium, stupour, and convulsions followed by a profound unconsciousness. In this condition the little sufferer had slept away. I refused to sign a death certificate, as I considered this death unjustifiable homicide, and a very proper one for the coroner to investigate.

Immense Abdominal Tumour in Christian Science Healer—Operation.

The enclosed photographs tell the story of the troubles of a Christian Science practitioner living on Sheridan Road, Chicago.

This woman was, and is a popular healer of this cult. However, for a period of seventeen months she was incapacitated by an abdominal tumour, which was too much for a regiment of healers. She came under my care at the A.... Hospital, and had her tumour removed surgically. She made an uneventful recovery, and is now once more engaged in the lucrative business of telling people that ailments are in their thought and nowhere else.

The photographs were taken at the time of the operation, and while the healer was snoring lustily under the influence of a material remedy, ether, that made her insensible to the knife. The first picture was taken just before the operation was begun, and the second shows what was left of the patient immediately after ninety pounds of tumour had been separated from her. These photographs were taken because this tumour was so enormous. In these days of watchfulness on the part of the medical profession, we seldom see such large tumours. These photographs are also conclusive evidence that this healer's truth and veracity are not of very high order, for even before she was well enough to leave the hospital she began claiming that her illness was all a mistake, and that in reality there had been no tumour.

Diabetes—Coma—Death.

There is a request in *Northwest Medicine* for October that readers of the journal mentioned who are familiar with cases in which favourable results could reasonably have been expected to follow the use of proper or surgical measures, but in which serious injury resulted through reliance on Christian Science, shall write reports of such cases.

This is the story of Mildred R., aged twelve, living at home with her father and mother. She had diabetes, was on the insulin treatment and getting along fairly well. Of course, insulin is not a cure for diabetes, and leaves much to be desired in the way of treatment for that disease. Mildred did not always follow her diet as she should, and often ate things she ought not to eat. Neither did she like a hypodermic injection of insulin before each meal, three times a day. But in spite of all this, she was getting along fairly well.

One day a lodge brother of her father's was at the house and told the usual story about a woman he once knew that was sick, and the doctors were not helping her at all, etc. This woman tried Christian Science and the next day she was well. Just like that. So Mildred decided that she wanted to try "Christian Science," and her father took her to a neighbouring town where one of these ladies lived and Mildred saw the Christian Science lady. The Eddyite told Mildred that she should discontinue the use of the insulin and she could eat anything she wanted to. Of course, this was joyful news to Mildred, and she immediately went down town and ate four ham sandwiches. That evening, at the picture show, Mildred was so sick that her father had to hire a taxicab to take her home. The next day she ate a big dinner, all she wanted, and she went into diabetic coma that night (Thursday) and died at 9 A. M. the following Saturday, October 4.

Acute Urinary Retention—Catheter Resorted to.

Not long since I was called, in a great hurry, to the home of one of the few Christian Scientists that infest this town. The occasion of this hurried call was the fact that the head of the family found himself unable to empty his bladder. The wife said to me: "Doctor, my husband is out of harmony, and we would like your help until we can heal him mentally." I found that this follower of Mary Baker Glover Patterson Eddy had, for twelve hours, been trying to convince himself that his bladder was not overloaded and that he was mistaken in thinking that the condition was becoming unbearable. The patient had been walking the floor with a copy of *Science and Health* in his hand till he could contain himself no longer. With a catheter I restored him to "harmony" in three minutes.

After drawing a long breath of relief, he delivered himself of the following: "What a fool I am? I would have been relieved if I had had faith and patience." Several times after that I piped off his disharmony with a catheter. Finally, he concluded that the Lord knew best, and accordingly he provided himself with a catheter of his own, and now when his bladder tries to interfere with his harmony he punctures the offending imaginary viscus with a hollow rubber tube, and thus proves the truth of Christian Science, and holds fast to that which is good.

Strangulated Hernia—At Christian Science Convention.

Miss J. F., aged thirty-two, single, went to Boston and attended a Christian Science convention. While there, a small lump appeared in the right femoral region, which caused pain and vomiting. The vomiting persisted, but she did not call a physician until the sixth day, when she was brought to the hospital by her relatives.

She was then delirious from absorption of the poisonous contents of the obstructed bowel. The hernia was operated upon, and the intestine in the hernial sac found gangrenous. The intestine was opened, and its toxic contents let out, but the patient never rallied; she died twenty-four hours after her admission to the hospital, her delirium never having subsided.

Peritonitis—Appendicitis—Abscess.

On the evening of March 21, 1923, I was called to see Florence, little daughter of J. W. Upon arriving at her bedside, I elicited the following history from the mother: The child had become ill about ten days previously with pain in its stomach, worse on the right side, it vomited and had some fever. A Christian Science practitioner was called the next day and came regularly each day for about five days. During this time there was no apparent change in the condition of the child. About the end of the fifth day the pain suddenly subsided, vomiting ceased and the child was apparently so much better that the practitioner next day pronounced her well, and told the parents she would not be back.

The child, however, evinced no desire to get up, but lay perfectly quiet in bed, and took no nourishment except a little water, which was retained. After a couple of days of this, the pain returned, and later the vomiting. These symptoms gradually increased in intensity up to the time I was called, three days afterwards. The healer had been recalled in the meantime, but her ministrations were of no avail.

Upon examining the child, I found a temperature of 102° F., a rapid thready pulse, a tense tympanitic abdomen so sensitive that the merest touch caused the child to cry out. The lower half of the abdomen was slightly dull on light percussion. The history was so clear-cut that deep palpation and percussion (which would have been very painful to the little patient) were not attempted—indeed, it did not seem necessary. It was plain that there had been an acute purulent infection of the appendix, which had burst open about the end of the fifth day, thus accounting for the temporary cessation of pain and vomiting. A little later, peritonitis developed, and at the time of the examination the lower abdomen was evidently filling up with pus.

I urged the immediate removal of the child to a hospital so that the abdomen could be opened, and the patient given the one chance she had left for her life. They would not consent to do so then, but said they would let me know in the morning. I did not hear from them until the morning of the second day thereafter, when they informed me they had decided to take her to a hospital. She was removed to the hospital, where the abdomen was opened, and, as we anticipated, found it full of pus—at least a quart of it—with diffuse peritonitis present. Drainage was established, and everything done to help maintain the little one's strength, but she gradually failed, and died on the third day after the operation.

*   *   *

Little more need be said on this topic of Christian Science "healing" and "cures," but it is wise to reflect that Mrs. Eddy herself knew the failures of her philosophy better than any one else, and lest she be called upon to demonstrate its shallow abilities, she inserted this footnote in her book, *Science and Health*:

The author takes no patients and declines medical consultation.[11]

One could hardly picture our Saviour turning away a repentant leper or even allowing Lazarus to remain in the grave, yet Mrs. Eddy, His self-proclaimed "successor," abruptly closed the door of her chamber of miracles to the faithful, and "declined" even to them the matchless privilege of consultation, that is to all but her household lackeys. What a testimony this is to the reputedly tenderhearted priestess of the Christian Science history books. But that was Mrs. Eddy, clever to the last, and beyond the comprehension or understanding of even her most intimate friends. It must never be forgotten that Mrs. Eddy once wrote:

A patient hears the doctor's verdict as the criminal hears his death sentence (*Science and Health*, p. 198).

Yet she made very real use of doctors for her spasmodic at-

---

[11]*The Faith, The Falsity, The Failure of Christian Science*, p. 337.

tacks of hysteria and toward the end of her life even allowed
Christian Scientists the right to use anesthetics,[12] surgery
and the services of bone doctors[13] for breaks and fractures,
etc., although she stoutly opposed such practices at the outset
of her career. However, no one can ever accuse Mrs. Eddy
of being a fool, since she seemingly made allowance for
some situations; but while she provided in a measure for the
bodies of her followers she left their souls poverty stricken,
barren and destitute, robbed of the true Christ and His gospel of life by one of her most pronounced delusions, the
alleged curative powers of Christian Science.

---

[12]*Science and Health,* p. 444.
[13]*Science and Health,* p. 401.

CHAPTER IX

CHRISTIAN SCIENCE OBJECTIONS

Some months after the publication of the second chapter of the first edition of this book, entitled "The Myth of Mother Eddy" (*Eternity* magazine, Jan., 1955), the authors encountered a polite but firm example of Christian Science opposition which we feel merits exposition in the interest of truth.

Eternity magazine[1] had published the chapter as an article in connection with the release of our book and in line with the convictions of its editorial staff that the problem of cults demands attention and concerned action on the part of Christians everywhere.

Shortly after the publication of said chapter, the head of the Christian Science Committee on Publication for the state of Pennsylvania, Mr. William V. K. Shepherd, called upon *Eternity* and politely criticized the article, stating that it contained "many errors in fact," and that it was "generally untrustworthy." Mr. Shepherd was interviewed at this time by Mr. Hitt, the Executive Editor, and Mr. Paul Hopkins, Executive Secretary of the Evangelical Foundation.

As a result of this meeting, Mr. Hitt agreed to arrange a meeting between Mr. Martin and Mr. Shepherd, to be held at the office of *Eternity* in Philadelphia, sometime during the ensuing month. At that meeting Mr. Shepherd very sharply criticized the article as it appeared in the magazine and the book itself. He displayed a well-marked and evidently thoroughly perused copy of the book.

During the course of the conference (which lasted five hours), Mr. Shepherd referred constantly to "valuable, re-

---

[1]Published by The Evangelical Foundation, Inc., 1716 Spruce Street, Philadelphia, Pennsylvania. Dr. Donald Grey Barnhouse, Editor; Russell T. Hitt, Executive Editor.

liable information available in Boston" which he claimed completely contradicted our book, and proved it false. At the close of the session, Mr. Martin agreed to meet anyone from the Boston headquarters who would come to New York and bring this "reliable evidence," and even offered to "retract anything that is proven to be a misrepresentation, and to apologize if the evidence warranted it."

On June 29, 1955, Mr. Martin received a letter from Mr. Shepherd in which he stated that the Christian Science Committees on Publication, in Boston, would contact him in the near future to arrange for a meeting at which "the evidence" discussed in Philadelphia would be forthcoming. Accompanying Mr. Shepherd's letter was a carbon copy of a letter sent to him by Mr. Will B. Davis, Manager of The Committees on Publication of the Christian Science Church, in which he scathingly attacked our book, and hazarded imputations relative to our motives, scholarship and intellectual integrity, among other things.

Since this letter was later found to contain the bulk of Christian Scientists' objections to *The Christian Science Myth,* we have decided to present choice examples of these alleged "refutations" so that the interested reader can judge for himself whether or not they are "reliable evidence" or whether they refute what we have written.

CHRISTIAN SCIENCE OBJECTIONS

(1.) Referring to: Page 12, *The Christian Science Myth* (1st edition). "Denying the principle that 'matter has reality,' Quimby built up a considerable following, having authored numerous pamphlets and manuscripts dealing with his theories."

Objection:

They cite *The Quimby Manuscripts* edited by Horatio Dresser, page 390, to the effect that "Dr. Quimby never uses the language of denial. He never explicitly says 'there is no matter', or 'there is no evil.' "

Answer:

On the surface this appears to disprove our statement completely, but the Scientists neglect to finish the quotation from Dresser which fully substantiates our claim. Mr. Dresser further said, in the next sentence: "This is a legitimate back-handed way of declaring what to him was the greatest truth; there is no reality save that which exists in God or Science. His realization of this truth was so strong that *he did not need denials*" (p. 390).

Our contention is that Quimby often spoke of matter in terms that challenged its "reality" (see *The Quimby Manuscripts,* pp. 137, 177, 295, 420, etc.). The Scientists are fully aware of this, and their attempt to deny it by giving only a partial quotation is most distressing, and scholastically dishonest.

(2.) Referring to: Page 12, *The Christian Science Myth* (1st edition). " 'Dr.' Quimby in the late 1850's had already discovered his 'Science of Man,' which manuscript was used by Mrs. Eddy and sections of which she copied and incorporated into 'her' textbook, *Science and Health, With Key to the Scriptures.*"

Objection:

The Scientists quote George Quimby, Dr. Quimby's son, in *The Quimby Manuscripts,* page 436, to the effect that "Mrs. Eddy had no access to father's manuscripts" (except *Questions and Answers*).

Answer:

The title page of the *Questions and Answers* manuscript Mrs. Eddy did have in Stoughton (1868-1870) bears the title "The Science of Man, or The Principle Which controls all

Phenomena" (see *The Quimby Manuscripts,* p. 438; also *The Religio-Medical Masquerade,* pp. 91-92).

We have not contended that this manuscript is the same[2] as Mrs. Eddy's later manuscript *Questions and Answers,* which bore the same title; we merely hold that she had Quimby's manuscript, as previously mentioned, and used it as source material.

(3.) Referring to: Page 12, *The Christian Science Myth* (1st edition). "Quimby's system was known as the 'Science of Christ.' "

Objection:

The Christian Science Church maintains that there is no evidence except in *The Quimby Manuscripts,* page 388, that Quimby ever used the term "Science of Christ."

Answer:

This is a rankly amateurish attempt to wriggle out of a nasty situation, especially so when we note that the Scientists had no objections to quoting *The Quimby Manuscripts* in attempting to refute us—see (1) and (2)—yet they now repudiate the same source they formerly quoted as authoritative! The fact of the matter is that Quimby did use the term "the Science of the Christ" in the article "Aristocracy and Democracy," February, 1863 (*The Quimby Manuscripts,* page 388) and this is prima facie evidence which the Scientists must disprove. This they must do not by denying it, but by showing evidence that will refute it, and this they have not done, nor do we believe they can.

(4.) Referring to: Page 14, *The Christian Science Myth* (1st edition). "Two incontrovertible facts establish these truths beyond doubt."

[2]*Mary Baker Eddy, The Truth and The Tradition,* E. S. Bates and J. V. Dittemore, p. 145.

Objection:

The Christian Scientists maintain that Dr. Cushing's statement about Mrs. Eddy is not true and that it was sworn to thirty years after its occurrence (see Clifford P. Smith, *Historical Sketches,* Chapter 7). They further maintain that we only partially quoted Mrs. Eddy's letter to Mr. Dresser, inferring that we did not give the complete picture or its context.

Answer:

Dr. Cushing was an extremely remarkable and methodical man who kept a record of his calls and the medicine administered throughout his entire practice, even though he often attended thirty or forty patients a day. His graphic account of Mrs. Eddy's fall on the ice, his treatment of her, and his comment, the statement he allegedly made that she would never walk again, etc., are all clearly set down in a lengthy affidavit, made when he was seventy-seven years old and in possession of all his faculties, and is based on his own case record book. Dr. Cushing refutes entirely Mrs. Eddy's entire story. It is unthinkable that he would deliberately swear falsely, whereas Mrs. Eddy has often been proved an untrustworthy witness. (See *The Life of Mary Baker G. Eddy and The History of Christian Science,* Georgine Milmine, pp. 84-86 for Dr. Cushing's affidavit.)

Attention should also be paid to Clifford P. Smith's attempt to "prove" that Mrs. Eddy was seriously injured in her fall on the ice where he quotes two witnesses (a newspaper clipping to the effect that she was badly injured is also part of their "evidence") who bolstered up Mrs. Eddy's claim. It should be remembered, however, that neither of these witnesses examined Mrs. Eddy, had any access to Dr. Cushing's diagnosis, or was competent to diagnose the extent of her injuries themselves. Their testimony or "evidence" is therefore totally worthless and an example of Christian Science

the "Bible Lessons" where the reference is alleged to have appeared. (As of this writing, the authors have found no such reference in the Bible Lessons of that period.) Instead, Mrs. Eddy named the new edition and requested all Scientists to read the paragraph as it appeared in that edition.

We feel justified in concluding, therefore, that she meant for them to "buy" and "sell" her book, not look it up in the elusive Bible Lesson, as our critics maintain. In the interest of clarity, however, we have reworded the sentence as it appears in this edition; but our contention is still the same, for unless her disciples bought the book, we find no evidence that they could have read the paragraph elsewhere, at least not at that time. If new evidence is forthcoming which would tend to disprove our statement, we will, of course, incorporate it in future editions.

(9.) Referring to Page 52, *The Christian Science Myth* (1st edition). "Since it is a fact questioned by no student of the movement's history that Mrs. Eddy claimed equality with Jesus, it follows that she should also claim for 'her' teachings divine revelation or equality with the Bible."

Objection:

The Christian Scientists vehemently deny that Mrs. Eddy ever claimed equality with Jesus, and contend further that there are students of the movement's history who disagree with our conclusions. Secondly, the Scientists challenge the quotation from Miss Milmine's book regarding Mrs. Eddy's claim to superiority for her "revelation" over the New Testament revelation, and imply that we have "plucked" the words out of context and even added six more. They maintain also that Mrs. Eddy herself denied equality with Christ and never claimed to be His successor (*The First Church of Christ Scientist, and Miscellany*, p. 129, etc.).

Answer:

(a) To be honest in his dealings with all men is one of the first duties of a Christian, and in keeping with this, we have removed in this edition the word "no" in reference to students of the Christian Science movement. We have used the word "few" instead, because there is a small minority who do hold that Mrs. Eddy never claimed equality with Christ.

However, if the interested reader will consult the *Christian Science Journal* for April of 1899, "Christ and Christmas" (poem), edition of 1894, the numerous references Mrs. Eddy makes in her writings to her "mission and actions" as God "impelled," and her acceptance of her book as that spoken of in the Tenth Chapter of The Apocalypse, verses 2 and 9 (*Science and Health,* ed. 1915, pp. 558, 559), we feel sure that it is amply in evidence that Mrs. Eddy at times claimed equality with Christ, which justifies our contention.

By way of further illustration, in the aforementioned poem, "Christ and Christmas," a picture of Christ, entitled "Christian Unity," pictures Him seated upon a stone holding a woman's hand. In her other hand, this woman holds a scroll entitled "Christian Science," and each of the figures, both Jesus and the woman, have bright halos conspicuously shining around their heads. The caption on the picture reads, "As in blessed Palestine's hour, so in our age, 'Tis the same hand unfolds His Power, and writes the Page."

If this picture does not convince any reasonably rational person that Mrs. Eddy pictured herself as that woman, complete with halo and *Science and Health* in her hand, then we question the value of any evidence introduced in the accepted category for evaluation.

Mrs. Eddy also believed that as Jesus suffered for the sins of others, so did she, and in a personal letter to D. H. Spofford in 1877 she made it only too clear. Wrote Mrs. Eddy:

" . . . those who call on me mentally in suffering are in belief kill-ing me! Stopping my work that none but me can do in their supreme selfishness . . . tell . . . them all it would be no greater crime for them to come directly and thrust a dagger into my heart, they are just as surely in belief killing me and committing murder. The sin lies at their door. . . . They lay on me suffering inconceivable" (Georgine Milmine, *The Life of Mary Baker G. Eddy And The History of Christian Science,* Doubleday, 1908, p. 214).

In the 1881 edition of *Science and Health,* Mrs. Eddy further displayed this concept when she wrote:

"In years past we suffered greatly for the sick when healing them, but even that is all over now, and we cannot suffer for them. But when we did suffer in belief, our joy was so great in removing others' sufferings that we bore ours cheerfully and willingly."

We leave the final decision in this matter to the reader who can judge for himself the validity of the Christian Science objections on this point of Mrs. Eddy's pretended equality with Jesus.

(b) It is also maintained by Mrs. Eddy's apologists that we "plucked" out of context her comment in a personal letter to a friend, to the effect that her revelation of Christian Science was, "higher, clearer and more permanent than before," and further that we even added six extra words in our quotation.

Regarding the addition of words, this was a typographical error, the words "higher," "clearer" and "more permanent" originally having been set off in quotation marks. In the setting of type, they were all run into one statement based upon the Milmine quotation found on page 494 of her book. This has been remedied, however, as can easily be seen from a brief glance at page 55, where the correct quote now appears.

Relative to the charge that we did not give the context of Mrs. Eddy's claim in the personal letter, we did not feel it was necessary. But since the Scientists doubt the sincerity of our motives, we shall quote it at this time.

"I know the crucifixion of the one who presents Truth in its higher aspect will be this time through a bigger error, through mortal mind instead of its lower strata or matter, showing that the idea given of God this time is higher, clearer and more permanent than before . . . you dear student are doubtless praying for me—and so the Modern Law giver is upheld for a time."[5]

From this quotation, one can easily see that Mrs. Eddy fancied herself the counterpart of Christ as the "Modern Law giver" who was anticipating crucifixion as "the one who presents Truth in its higher aspect." This crucifixion was to be "through mortal mind instead of through its lower strata or matter" (Jesus on the Cross) and is clearly self-applied by Mrs. Eddy. Such a statement leaves little doubt as to what her opinion of herself and her "revelation" was, and certainly explodes the fantasy that she never claimed equality with the Lord Jesus.

In summing up these Christian Science objections and our answers, we think it proper to say that we have attempted to deal honestly and judiciously with the criticisms of our sometimes unkind antagonists. The small percentage of historical errors they have been able to filter out of the book, we feel justifies our claim that in almost 98 per cent of all the instances cited, the material altered has not changed the facts or the picture we have presented, nor has it affected in one iota the over-all veracity or dependability of the book. The authors admit that all books are subject to some margin of error and freely own their personal mortal frailty in such cases. But essentially we hold that this book tells the whole truth about one of the world's worst and most clever pseudo-Christian masquerades, whose numerous, ever-smiling emissaries can never change the fact that their religion denies The Core of Christianity; The Book, The Blood and The Blessed Hope. This system, then, finds no justification linguistically, historically or Biblically for its theology, which is the product of unlearned female prestidigitation and the hallucinations of Mary Baker Eddy.

---

[5]Georgine Milmine, *The Life of Mary Baker G. Eddy*, etc., p. 73.

AUTHOR'S NOTE: Some weeks after Mr. Martin's meeting with Mr. Shepherd, he received a telephone call from Mr. Robert Peel, Chief of The Editorial Section of The Christian Science Church's Committees on Publications, who requested an interview in New York to discuss our book. Mr. Martin agreed to the meeting and an appointment was made.

The authors met Mr. Peel in New York, in his room at the Hotel Commodore and had two enjoyable days to review the major objections to our book. At these meetings Mr. Peel failed to introduce any "new" evidence which disproved in any way our major contention in the book, and we have covered quite thoroughly in the text of this chapter virtually all he had to offer.

CHAPTER X

THE CHALLENGE OF CULTISM

The last one hundred and thirty years have been most fruitful ones for both the founding and development of cultism in America. From relatively small beginnings major cults have developed into such enormous proportions as to present a genuine threat to all Christendom and more particularly to the orthodox interpretation of the Bible. Due to their shrewd emphasis on advertising and printed propaganda, the cults have far outstripped evangelical Christianity in the field of personal work, preferring to reach the person as an individual and thus better instill their peculiar beliefs. Jehovah's Witnesses,[1] for instance, have greatly capitalized on the New Testament command to go out by two's, and may be seen advancing their Theocratic Kingdom daily the world over. It is helpful to remember, as you deal with cultists no matter what type they adhere to, that cults are almost always built, not upon Scripture, but upon a particular person's *interpretation* of Scripture,[2] so that in the final analysis one must cope with their founder's theological interpretation in order to undermine faith in the related cult.

Christian Science being another of the major cults which plague evangelical efforts, therefore it, too, merits comment. Upon the demise of Mary Baker Eddy ("Mother" to the faithful) in 1910 and the subsequent failure of her most earnest disciples' hope that she, like Jesus Christ, would rise from the dead, Christian Science, instead of dying out as was

[1]This cult began with Charles Taze Russell in 1871. Russell rejected the doctrine of hell and eternal retribution and founded his cult as a protest against all organized religion.
[2]Witness—Joseph Smith, Mormonism; Mary Baker Eddy—Christian Science; C. T. Russell—Jehovah's Witnesses.

so disastrously anticipated by its adversaries, has multiplied
into alarming proportions which are too large to be ignored
any longer. To be sure, many books and pamphlets have
been written on Christian Science and its founder, but these
are all for the most part gathering dust on long-forgotten
library shelves and in attics while the myth of "Mother" Eddy
flourishes virtually unchallenged and apparently unimpeded.
In all truth there does not exist today, to the authors' knowledge, any modern (within the last 20 years) historical
or theological refutations that the interested pastor, teacher
or layman can read and quote authoritatively against the
followers of Mrs. Eddy, or for that matter, any of the major
cults.[3] Most certainly there are chapters in certain specialized
textbooks which are good, but none sufficiently documentary
as to be completely reliable, and in most cases badly out-
dated. In order to squarely meet the challenge of cultism
today (and make no mistake, it is a real challenge of no
small proportions), Christians must above all else be accurate
in their evaluations, consistent in their theology and exhaustively patient in their approach to cult adherents. Let
us not make the mistake of forcing the gospel upon anyone,
or attempting to force a person against his or her will to
accept doctrines which we do not take time to give adequate
Scriptural ground for believing. St. Peter, writing in his first
epistle, adjures us to be able to give to everyone that asks of us
a reason for the hope that is in us—which we know to be Christ
—the hope of Glory. Nothing is gained by unexplained dog-
matism, but patient explanations of Scriptural truths, no matter how often repeated, will bear much more fruit spiritually in the end than abrupt dismissals of foreign doctrines
as "of the devil!" Today more than ever before, we must, as
a united Christian effort, take a united stand against the cults
of all varieties; we dare not wait any longer. The attractive-

---

[3]*Jehovah of The Watchtower* and *The Christian Science Myth* are the only two
exceptions.

ness of Christian Science lies in its seeming power over disease and mental conflict, but to quote Psychologist David S. Davis: "What has been induced by suggestion can be cured by suggestion."[4]

Most illnesses "cured" by Christian Scientists are imagined illnesses which lack medical documentation and are seldom thoroughly verified by anyone other than the Scientists or their sympathizers. The physical world to most Christian Scientists is an "illusion of mortal mind," but they are quick to seize every opportunity to avail themselves of all the comforts this same "mortal mind" conjures up.

With this philosophy it is easy to see how even sin, with all its hideousness, is reduced to a state of mind, and death to a flighty "illusion."

Since the central doctrine of almost all cults is the denial of both the Deity and Saviourhood of the Lord Jesus, we must exert renewed effort in preaching and teaching these major doctrines of our Christian heritage. We must be quick to expose error and even still quicker to extend to all cultists the love of God and the assurance of forgiveness through His Eternal Son, if they will but come to the Christ of Calvary.

Let us not forget, however, that Christian Science can temporarily impute peace of mind, and this cannot be doubted; but, that it is able to cure "diagnosed diseases," give peace of soul, or most of all, peace with God, is a question to which the Bible emphatically says—No! The Bible clearly teaches that salvation is effected solely through the Grace of God as revealed in Jesus Christ and His substitutionary atonement on the cross. The Christ of Christianity is a Personality—God Incarnate (John 1:1-14)—not the "Divine Idea" of a pantheistic nonentity, as Mrs. Eddy has portrayed Him to be.

It is therefore important to remember that Mrs. Eddy never believed in a Personal God nor does any true Christian

---

[4] Prof. David S. Davis, *A Psychologist Views the Cults*, from *The Examiner*, Vol I, January-February No. 1, p. 11.

Scientist today. Mrs. Eddy's last words, which she scrawled with a trembling hand on a scrap of paper shortly before her death, "God is my life," might just as well have read, "Principle, Love, Spirit, or Intelligence is my life." To her utterly confused mind the God of the Bible did not exist; for her, God was not personal in any sense, since her limited theology only permitted an "It" which was "all in all." Aside from adoring this pantheistic, impersonal deity, Mrs. Eddy, and consequently all Christian Scientist practitioners today, expound this concept as the Master Key to all human misery. Paradoxically, however, they deny misery exists in the first place but never tire of trying to convince anyone who will listen, for a handsome fee, that Christian Science can remove this "error of mortal mind" through "prayer." The great byword of Christian Science, incidentally, is "prayer," and they never cease reminding their audience that they always pray to "God" for healing. But is it really prayer? The Scriptures teach that prayer is one's petition to a personal God who sees our needs and answers them (Phil. 4:6, 7). Not so in Christian Science. Mrs. Eddy many times reaffirmed her conviction that prayer to a personal God is a hindrance, not a help. To her and Christian Science the only true prayer is "the affirmation of Principle's Allness" and the identification of one's self with this pantheistic Principle. From this basic misconception stems the illusion of man's inherent goodness and the denial of the "erroneous" idea that evil, or for that matter, sin, suffering, disease, or even death, is real. With this view of life it is easy to see how Christian Scientists can appear so apparently happy and oblivious to everyday worries. Whenever they encounter evil they deny its reality; whenever they behold misery, they affirm its nonexistence; and even when death comes to a loved one, they simply assert that it is an "illusion" since Principle (God) is All, and "It" is *good* (?).

It would be possible to go on indefinitely with the many strange interpretations which Mrs. Eddy gave to the Scriptures.

However, suffice it to say, that she never believed in them as God's infallible Word, nor worshipped the Saviour within its pages. The Christian's most holy and sacred doctrine of love, which is Christ crucified for us and His sacrificial blood our atonement with God, Mrs. Eddy abruptly dismissed as unnecessary. She equally ignored the existence of hell, Satan, or, for that matter, a literal heaven. (For her it was a "state of mind.") Nowhere in the annals of cultism is there to be found a person who camouflaged so expertly the "broad way of destruction" under a canopy of apparent serenity as did Mary Baker Eddy. Nevertheless, beneath this "serenity" lies a clever denial of all orthodox Christianity.

The Christ of the Bible is a real Person and a living Saviour who openly recognized the existence and reality of sin, disease, and death. Jesus always actively combated them with personal divine power. He never ignored their reality. The Christ of Christian Science is merely an "Idea," which cannot save, and there is salvation in no other but the Eternal Word made Flesh (John 1:14). Therefore, let us clearly distinguish between the God of the Bible and the "It" of Mrs. Eddy. Let us declare the Christ of Calvary in opposition to the "Divine Idea" of Christian Science. And, finally, let us understand the difference between the salvation of God and the saturation of *Science and Health*. Christian Science comes in the wisdom of the world and the clothing of sheep, but never in the power of God, and we know that "The world by wisdom knew not God" (I Cor. 1:21).

In concluding this survey of Mrs. Eddy's religion, it is extremely important that the implications of Christian Science be thoroughly understood by Christians and non-Christians alike. It is important for Christians because ignorance of Christian Science has been one of the main contributing factors to the success of its rapid development. For non-Christians it is important because it is a cunning and subtle counterfeit of the true gospel which bears no resemblance whatsoever to the doctrines of Jesus Christ and cannot in any sense free the soul from the power of guilt and sin.

As Russellism (Jehovah's Witnesses) feeds upon the personality that desires importance and a false sense of Biblical knowledge, so Christian Science preys upon the intellectually-proud mind—the intellect that desires above all else freedom from the fear of ill health, and justification for personal sin that is conveniently denied by Mrs. Eddy. All in all it is a fascinating study unrivaled in the history of cultism and one that ought to stimulate the greatest of efforts in the lives of awakened Christian people everywhere. To the average Christian Scientist there is no sin. Whatever he does that is adjudged wrong by human standards is denied as "error," and the machinations of Mrs. Eddy's devil, Malicious Animal Magnetism. No Christian Scientist the authors have ever met will admit that he sins against the character and laws of a holy God and must either repent or be punished eternally. There is no true follower of the Eddy religion who will allow the possibility that the God of the Bible will punish him for his unbelief, and safe in this delusion Christian Scientists delight in affirming Mrs. Eddy's meaningless syllogisms over against the Word of God.

Many good people often comment on the buoyant attitude of Christian Scientists in general and the fact that they are happy in their religion and seemingly hinder no one else's. However, this is not the complete picture, nor is it by any means the whole truth where Christian Science is concerned. To begin with, Christian Science theology, as has been fully shown, is a direct opposite of Christianity and the avowed enemy of Biblical theology. Christian Scientists are happy, it is true, but this mask of happiness disappears when cancer, tuberculosis, heart disease and sudden death daily challenge the validity of the Eddy philosophy. The Bible teaches us that Christ came into the world to save sinners (I Tim. 1:15), but Christian Scientists are so consistently self-righteous and proud that they deny not only their own guilt of sin but the very existence of evil itself. Not long ago one of the authors had occasion to speak at length with a well-educated young woman, herself a devout Christian Scientist and her mother a practitioner. During the course of the conversation and in answer to his statement that Jesus died on the cross for her sins to give her life eternal in a real heaven, not a state of mind, and further, that His blood was shed to save her and bring her to perfection, she unashamedly replied in tones of near flippancy:

There was no need for Jesus to climb up on any cross and die for me; I am already perfect, for I am the reflection of the Divine Idea.

Without fear of contradiction we may boldly say that with small modification this statement in substance is the logical conclusion to which all Christian Scientists are driven because Mrs. Eddy fostered and perpetrated the concept long before they ever dreamed of accepting it. Mrs. Eddy herself cared little whether Jesus ever lived, much less died, and this is not an overstatement, it is merely a little-known fact. Mrs. Eddy said to the Rev. James Henry Wiggin, her literary adviser:

If there had never existed such a person as the Galilean prophet it would make no difference to me. I should still know that God's spiritual ideal is the only real man in his image and likeness.[5]

But above and beyond the vagaries of Mrs. Eddy, one problem is paramount in the theology of Christian Science, and that is, can Christian Science do what it says it can? Does it protect its members from disease, sickness and death? Are Christian Scientists really any different physically than anyone else? Are they immune to suffering? To all of these questions the answer is an unequivocable *No.* Christian Science cannot halt the processes of physical decay and in this sense they are no different than anyone else. An eminent

---

[5]*The First Church of Christ, Scientist and Miscellany,* Mary Baker Eddy, pp. 318-319.

dentist once told the authors during a conversation dealing with Christian Science that some of his best patients were Christian Scientists who never flinched at the injection of novocaine and had just as many cavities and sets of false teeth as anyone else. He chuckled wryly when he said:

> They may be able to cure many of the things they say they can, but I have never met one yet that could think himself out of a good old-fashioned toothache.

Mrs. Eddy herself died toothless despite her numerous protestations that disease, decay and death were illusions. She was careful, however, to always make use of false teeth and eventually took them with her to a grave she denied had power over the body she insisted was imaginary. But be that as it may, Mary Baker Eddy is very, very dead and even the wailings of her foremost disciple, Augusta E. Stetson, could not resuscitate the emaciated form of the prophetess of Christian Science. All of the testimonials to alleged Christian Science healings can never belie the cold, unalterable fact that those who follow the Eddy Myth suffer like anyone else, feel pain like other mortals, and die the same death of physical dissolution that they so vehemently deny.

Another of the underlying attractions of Christian Science which no doubt accounts for its growing membership is the fact that in our age of scientific advancement and the subsequent emphasis on science, people like to think of themselves as scientists or philosophers of one sort or another. In the ranks of Christian Science, the trained eye may therefore discern the picture of thousands of ill-informed and badly deceived persons calling themselves "Scientists" and enjoying the title of "Metaphysicians." This is indeed a subtle appeal, an opportunity to be a philosopher, theologian and healer all rolled into one package, no experience necessary, cash on the barrelhead and health unlimited—apply at the nearest Christian Science business office. For prompt service have a large bank account and good financial references available.

In the words of F. W. Peabody, the noted Boston lawyer and contemporary antagonist of Mrs. Eddy:

> Highwaymen demand "your money or your life!" Christian Science, beguiling with siren smile, deluding with false promise, takes your money and your life! Instead of abolishing sin, sickness and death, Christian Science makes very substantial contributions to all three.[6]

The propaganda efforts of Christian Scientists are also unceasing and tireless in their operation and their overly polite invitation, "Why not try Science?" has become a stock phrase no longer carrying the connotation of spiritual death so prominent in its early evolutionary period. Fifty years ago Christian Science was unmasked as the clever counterfeit of Christianity that it is, and numerous books and pamphlets circulated freely warning of its spiritual and physical menace. Today, due to the various methods of suppression utilized by Christian Science pressure groups in the past, these works are all virtually out of circulation, and even libraries do not generally have them listed as available unless specifically requested. Mrs. Eddy's publicity committees have done their task well, and they have been aided in no small measure by the attitude all too common in Christian circles that cults are "not important" and "do not merit intense counter measures." Christian Science radio programs also abound throughout the length and breadth of America tirelessly filling the ether waves with the "God is Love—Love is God" propaganda that sounds wonderful to the untrained ear. This type of approach especially appeals to those who do not know that Mrs. Eddy's god and the god of Christian Science is not the God of the Bible, and that the Christ of Christian Science is a meaningless symbol for the ancient Gnostic heresy so prominent in the first century of the Christian church. On the outside, Christian Science verily appears as a saviour from sickness and ill health, an easy religion to follow be-

[6]*The Faith, Falsity and Failure of Christian Science*, pp. 339, 403.

cause it demands nothing of the soul but blind obedience and homage to Mary Baker Eddy and her textbook. The powers that rule Christian Sciencedom profit yearly from their high positions on a salary basis, and the numerous Christian Science practitioners who repeatedly tell sick, injured and dying men, women and children that "matter is an illusion" and hence they are not suffering, derive much from their lucrative practices. As Dr. Morris Fishbein of the American Medical Association once put it:

> I am still more concerned with the adult's custodianship of the body of the child. And how many children have had their lives ruined by this Christian Science insistence that pain is merely a figment of the imagination, no one can estimate. The tale has been told in a variety of manners: bitterly, by the surviving relatives of some child or too trusting believer who passed by this Christian Science route— a direct express—to the unknown land beyond life; . . . relentlessly, by physicians and by ministers who have seen needless deaths and suffering; revengefully, by lawyers of those who have hated to see hard-won wealth pass into the hands of suave healers and boards of management.[7]

With the conclusions of Dr. Fishbein all intelligent men and women will doubtless agree, but agreement is not enough. Evangelical Christianity has too long neglected the field of cults and the results of that failure face us today on every street corner and mission field of the world. Now more than ever we must realize that it is not *what* we believe, for this is a matter of common record, but *why* we believe it and why we must be prepared to *defend it vigorously*. There are two great commandments in the New Testament; one is known almost universally by all true Christians—it is "Preach the Word" (II Tim. 4:2). The other, sad to say, remains badly neglected by a great majority of Christian leaders and lay-men. It is "contend for the faith" (Jude 3), "reprove, rebuke, exhort with all longsuffering and doctrine" (II Tim. 4:2). The majority of St. Paul's epistles were doctrinal in nature

---

[7]Morris Fishbein, "Plain Talk Magazine," Vol. I, No. 2, November, 1927, pp. 14-26.

and apologetic in character; can we afford to be less faithful in our age to the same challenge than he was in his? We cannot; we dare not; the need is too urgent. We would all do well to follow the example of the greatest of apostles, missionaries and evangelists who commanded us in the name of our Saviour to "reprove" and "rebuke" error vigorously wherever it appears and under whatever colors it disguises itself. God grant that many consecrated Christians will rise to the standard of a polemical ministry dedicated in a spirit of Christian love to the reproving of doctrinal error and the personal defense of our Lord Jesus Christ.

It is the hope and prayer of the authors that the Lord may presently see fit to enrich this ministry with alert and aroused brethren who will not flinch at the uncomfortable odds, and who will loyally "contend for the faith once delivered unto the saints."

May the Lord, who is rich in mercy, open the eyes of His people to this mighty challenge when it shall best please Him, and may He be pleased to reveal through this book to any and all Christian Scientists who may read it, the empty and shallow pretenses of Mrs. Eddy, and the utter falsehood of her religion—which has become "The Christian Science Myth."

BIBLIOGRAPHY

I. Writings by Mary Baker Eddy

Science and Health, With Key to the Scriptures
Miscellaneous Writings
Manual of the Mother Church
Christ and Christmas
Retrospection and Introspection
Unity of Good
Pulpit and Press
Rudimental Divine Science
No and Yes
Christian Science Versus Pantheism
Message to the Mother Church, June, 1900
Message to the Mother Church, June, 1901
Message to the Mother Church, June, 1902
Christian Healing
The Peoples' Idea of God
Poems
The First Church of Christ, Scientist, and Miscellany
Christian Science Hymnal, with five hymns written by Mary Baker Eddy,
    C.S.P.S.,[1] 1909

II. Additional General Bibliography

A Complete Concordance to the Writings of Mary Baker Eddy Other
    Than Science and Health
A Complete Concordance to Science and Health, With Key to the
    Scriptures
The Christian Science Journal—Assorted Copies
The Christian Science Sentinel—Assorted Copies
The Christian Science Monitor—Assorted Copies
ARMSTRONG, JOSEPH, The Mother Church, C.S.P.S., 1937.
BATES, ERNEST SUTHERLAND and DITTEMORE, JOHN V., Mary Baker Eddy—
    The Truth and The Tradition, Alfred A. Knopf, 1932.
BEASLEY, NORMAN, The Cross and The Crown, The History of Christian
    Science, Duell, Sloan & Pearce, 1952.

---

[1]Christian Science Publishing Society.

BOLTZLY, REV. OLIVER D., *The Death Pot in Christian Science*, The Lutheran Literary Board, 1935.

DAKIN, EDWIN FRANDEN, *Mrs. Eddy*, Charles Scribner's & Sons, 1929.

DICKEY, ADAM, *Memoirs of Mary Baker Eddy*, Robert G. Carter, England, 1927.

DOUGLASS, R. C., *Christian Science, A Defense*.

DRESSER, HORATIO W. (edited by), *The Quimby Manuscripts*, Thomas Y. Crowell Co., 1921, first edition.

HALDEMAN, ISAAC MASSEY, *Christian Science in the Light of Holy Scripture*, Fleming H. Revell Co., 1909.

HANNA, SEPTIMUS J., *Christian Science History*, C.S.P.S., 1899.

HAWKINS, ANN BALLEW, *Phineas Parkhurst Quimby* (published by the author), 1951.

JOHNSTON, JULIA MICHAEL, *Mary Baker Eddy, Her Mission and Triumph*, C.S.P.S., 1946.

MILMINE, GEORGINE, *The Life of Mary Baker Eddy and The History of Christian Science*, Doubleday Page & Co., 1909.

MOORE, REV. A. LINCOLN, *Christian Science—Its Manifold Attraction*, Theodore E. Schulte Publishing Co., 1906.

PAGET, STEPHEN, M.D., *The Faith and Works of Christian Science*, London, 1909.

PEABODY, FREDERICK W., *The Religio-Medical Masquerade*, Fleming H. Revell Co., 1910.

PHILIPS, JANE, *Mary Baker Eddy's Early Writings Compared With The Quimby Manuscripts*, Toujours Publishing Co., Pasadena, California, 1931.

POWELL, LYMAN P., *Mary Baker Eddy*, MacMillan Co., 1930.

RAMSAY, E. MARY, *Christian Science and Its Discoverer*, C.S.P.S., 1935.

RIDDLE, T. WILKINSON, *Christian Science in the Light of Holy Scripture*, Marshall, Morgan and Scott, London, 1931.

RILEY, WOODBRIDGE; PEABODY, W. FREDERICK; and HUMISTON, CHARLES E., *The Faith, The Falsity and the Failure of Christian Science*, Fleming H. Revell Co., 1925.

SHELDON, HENRY C., *Christian Science So-Called*, The Abingdon Press, 1913.

SMITH, CLIFFORD P., *Historical Sketches*, C.S.P.S., 1941.

SNOWDEN, JAMES H., *The Truth About Christian Science*, Westminster Press, 1920.

STEWART, HERBERT, *Christian Science—True or False*, Graham L. Healy, Ltd., Belfast.

TENNEY, REV. HERBERT MELVILLE, *Christian Science, Its Truths and Errors*, The Burrows Brothers Co., 1888.

TOMLINSON, IRVING C., *Twelve Years With Mary Baker Eddy*, C.S.P.S., 1945.

TWAIN, MARK, *Christian Science*, Harper & Brothers, 1907.

WILBUR, SIBYL, *The Life of Mary Baker Eddy*, C.S.P.S., 1923.

WILLIAMSON, MARGARET, *The Mother Church Extension,* C.S.P.S., 1939.
WITTMER, GEORGE W., *Christian Science in the Light of the Bible,* Concordia Publishing House, 1949.
Christian Science Wartime Activities, 1939-1947, C.S.P.S.
Legal Aspects of Christian Science, 1899, C.S.P.S.

III. Newspaper and Magazine Articles, and Selected Chapters from Specialized Books

"100 Christian Science Cures," by Richard C. Cabot, M.D., *McClures Magazine,* August, 1908.
"Mary Baker Eddy," by Morris Fishbein, M.D., *Plain Talk,* Vol. 1, No. 2, November, 1927 (pp. 21-26).
"Dr. J. M. Buckley on Christian Science," by Dr. J. M. Buckley, *North American Review,* July, 1901.
"How Reverend Wiggin Rewrote Mrs. Eddy's Book," by Livingstone Wright, *New York World.*
"Quimbyism or the Paternity of Christian Science," by Josephine C. Woodbury, *Arena,* May, 1899.
"*War in Heaven,*" by Josephine C. Woodbury, S. Usher Printer, Boston, 1897.
"The Deadly Parallel," *New York Times,* July 10, 1904.
"Was Mrs. Eddy A Plagiarist?," *Current Opinion,* May, 1922.
FERGUSON, CHARLES W., *The New Books of Revelation* (Chapter on Christian Science), Doubleday Doran and Co., 1929.
GRAY, JAMES M., *The Antidote to Christian Science,* Moody Press, Chicago.
HADDEN, ROBERT A., *Christian Science and the Christian Scriptures Compared and Contrasted,* American Prophetic League, 1952.
MEEKAN, M., *Mrs. Eddy and the Late Suit in Equity,* Concord, 1908.
VAN BAALEN, J. K., *The Chaos of Cults* (Chapter on Christian Science), W. B. Eerdmans Co., 1951.
Arena Magazine, Selected copy regarding Mrs. Eddy and Christian Science.
McClures Magazine, Selected copy regarding Mrs. Eddy and Christian Science.
Religion in the Twentieth Century (Chapter on Christian Science), edited by Vergilus Ferm, Philosophical Library, 1948.
The Blight That Failed, Charles Scribner's Sons, 1929.
The New York Herald Tribune, Article and editorial on Christian Science, December 12 and 13, 1951.
The New York Times, Selected material on Christian Science, etc.
The New York World, Selected material on Christian Science, etc.

IV. SYSTEMATIC THEOLOGICAL AND PHILOSOPHICAL
REFERENCE WORKS BEARING ON CHRISTIAN SCIENCE

The Ancient World and Christianity, E. DePressense, A. C. Armstrong & Son.

A History of the Christian Church, Lars Qualben, Thomas Nelson & Sons, 1942.

The Ante and Post Nicene Fathers, Selected chapters.

International Standard Bible Encyclopedia.

Encyclopedia Britannica, "Mary Baker Eddy and Christian Science."

Treasure House of the Living Religions, Robert Ernest Hume, Charles Scribner's Sons, 1933.

History of the Christian Church, Philip Schaff.

Life and Epistles of the Apostle Paul, W. J. Conybeare and J. S. Howson, Thomas Y. Crowell & Co.

The Origin of Paul's Religion, J. Gresham Machen, William B. Eerdmans Co., 1947.

The Virgin Birth of Christ, J. Gresham Machen, Harper & Brothers, 1930.

The Life and Work of St. Paul, F. W. Farrar, E. P. Dutton & Co., 1879.

An Introduction to Christian Apologetics, Edward J. Carnell, Wm. B. Eerdmans, 1945.

A Philosophy of the Christian Religion, Edward J. Carnell, Wm. B. Eerdmans, 1952.

Systematic Theology, Vol. I, II, III, Charles Hodge, Wm. B. Eerdmans, 1946.

Systematic Theology, Vol. I, II, III, Augustus H. Strong, Judson Press, 1951.

The Person and Work of Christ, Benjamin Breckenridge Warfield, The Presbyterian and Reformed Publishing Co., 1950.

Basic Writings of St. Augustine (2 Volumes), Edited by Pegis, Random House, 1950.

Basic Writings of St. Thomas Aquinas (2 Volumes), Edited By Pegis, Random House, 1950.

History of Philosophy, B. A. G. Fuller, Henry Holt & Co., 1950.

Twentieth Century Philosophy, Edited by Dagobert D. Runes, Philosophical Library, 1947.

The Dictionary of Philosophy, Edited by Dagobert D. Runes, Philosophical Library, 1951.

Philosophy of Religion, John A. Nicholson, The Ronald Press Co., 1950.

Thayer's Greek-English Lexicon of the New Testament, Joseph H. Thayer, American Book Co., 1952.

Strong's Exhaustive Concordance of the Bible, James Strong, Abingdon-Cokesbury Press, 1951.

Gesenius, Hebrew and Chaldee Lexicon to the Old Testament, translated by S. P. Tregelles, Wm. B. Eerdmans Co., 1949.

Critical Thinking, Max Black, Prentice-Hall Inc., 1949 (Logic and Scientific Method).

Ethical Theories, Edited by A. I. Melden, Prentice-Hall Inc., 1950.

The Religions of the World, Godfrey E. Phillips, The Religious Education Press, 1948.

The Light in Dark Ages, V. Raymond Edman, Van Kampen Press, 1949.

Biblical Demonology, Merrill F. Unger, Van Kampen Press, 1952.

Therefore Stand, Wilbur M. Smith, W. A. Wilde Co., 1945.

"The Bible in Christian Science Literature," by Wilbur M. Smith, Sunday School Times Co., February 9, 1952.

The Leaven of the Sadducees, Ernest Gordon, The Bible Institute Colportage Assn., 1926.

Handbook of the Denominations in the United States, Frank S. Mead, Abingdon-Cokesbury Press, 1951.

V. BIBLICAL TRANSLATION

King James, Authorized Version of the Bible.

American Standard Version of the Bible.

Revised Standard Version of the Bible, National Council of Christian Churches.

Williams' Translation of the New Testament, Charles Williams.

Knox's Translation of the Bible, Monsignor Ronald Knox (Roman Catholic).

Douay-Rheims Version of the Bible (Roman Catholic).

INDEX